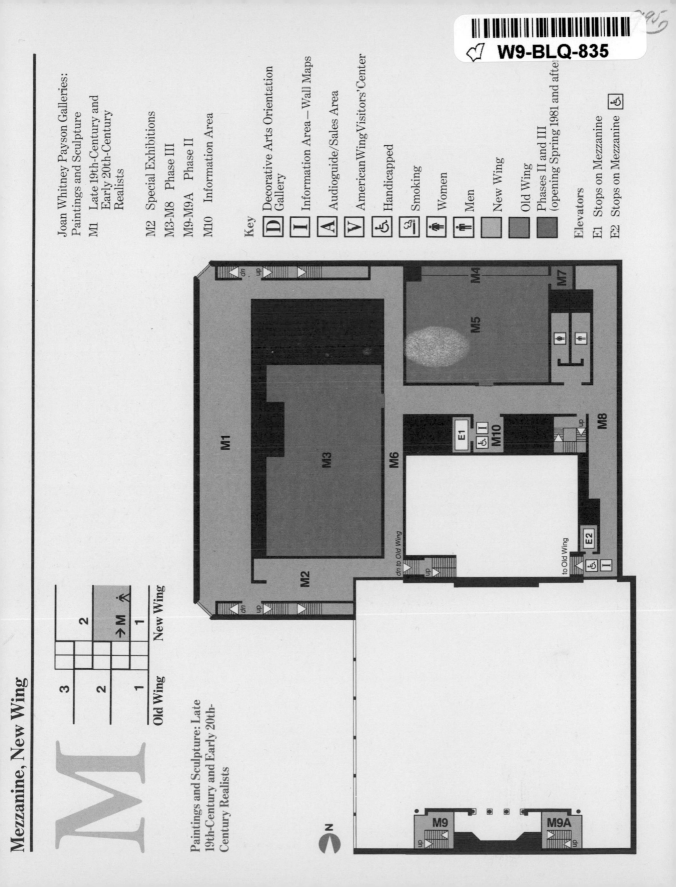

Mezzanine, New Wing

Paintings and Sculpture: Late 19th-Century and Early 20th-Century Realists

Old Wing · New Wing

Joan Whitney Payson Galleries: Paintings and Sculpture

M1 Late 19th-Century and Early 20th-Century Realists

M2 Special Exhibitions

M3-M8 Phase III

M9-M9A Phase II

M10 Information Area

Key

D Decorative Arts Orientation Gallery

I Information Area – Wall Maps

A Audioguide/Sales Area

V American Wing Visitors' Center

[wheelchair] Handicapped

[smoking] Smoking

[women] Women

[men] Men

New Wing

Old Wing

Phases II and III (opening Spring 1981 and after)

Elevators

E1 Stops on Mezzanine

E2 Stops on Mezzanine [wheelchair]

THE AMERICAN
WING / *A GUIDE*

THE AMERICAN WING *A Guide*

By MARSHALL B. DAVIDSON

The Metropolitan Museum of Art

NEW YORK

FRONTISPIECE: *Northeaster,* by Winslow Homer (1836-1910), oil on canvas, 34⅜ by 50¼ inches, 1895.
Gift of George A. Hearn, 10.64.5

ON THE COVER: marble façade of the United States Branch Bank, built by Martin E. Thompson in 1822-1824. It was originally located at 15½ Wall Street, New York City.
Gift of Robert W. de Forest, 1924.

PUBLISHED BY
The Metropolitan Museum of Art, New York
Bradford D. Kelleher, Publisher
John P. O'Neill, Editor in Chief
Elizabeth Stillinger, Editor
Peter Oldenburg, Designer

Cover Photograph by Stan Ries. *Floor Plans by* DeMartin, Marona, Cranstoun, Downes. *Garden Court Plans by* Joseph Ascherl. *Composed by* Finn Typographic Service, Inc., Stamford, Connecticut. *Printed by* Colorcraft Offset, Inc., New York. *Bound by* Mueller Trade Bindery, Inc., Middletown, Connecticut.

ISBN 0-87099-238-4

Library of Congress Catalogue Number: 80-7800

CONTENTS

COLOR PLATES

FOREWORD

The collection of American art at the Metropolitan Museum is one of the most comprehensive in the United States. Owing to the strong support of such early Trustees as Frederic Church, Eastman Johnson, and John F. Kensett—all renowned artists—American paintings and sculpture were prominent in the Museum's collections from the beginning.

In 1872, the Museum acquired its first American sculpture, an allegorical female nude by Hiram Powers entitled *California*. Shortly afterward a group of unfinished landscapes by the late John F. Kensett was given by the artist's brother, providing the beginnings of one of the department's strengths—Hudson River school paintings of the late nineteenth century. From this formative period onward, the collection was actively expanded through gifts and purchases. Each major loan exhibition held at the Museum created impetus for further growth.

In the field of decorative arts, the first major event was the large exhibition of American furniture, silver, glass, and paintings held in connection with the Hudson-Fulton Celebration of 1909. This landmark exhibit marked the first time that an art museum had shown American decorative and fine arts together in an orderly, chronological display. As a result of the overwhelmingly positive response to the Hudson-Fulton show, Mrs. Russell Sage purchased the distinguished Bolles collection of early American furniture and other objects for presentation to the Museum. This group of nearly 900 items, many of which had been on exhibition during the Hudson-Fulton Celebration, became the nucleus of the American Wing collection.

Major recognition of the importance of the American art collection, however, came with the creation of a separate wing largely devoted to period rooms. Opened in 1924 through the generosity and foresight of Robert W. de Forest, then the Museum's president, this highly innovative installation set a precedent in the display of American decorative arts. Three periods from the seventeenth through the early nineteenth century were represented in about twenty rooms with interior woodwork from old American houses. The installation had a profound influence on attitudes toward American art throughout the country—it affected the art market, individual collectors, installations in other museums, and American studies in the academic world.

Now, with the spacious additions recently designed by Kevin Roche and John Dinkeloo, a great part of the collection will be on display—an enviable feat in view of the Metropolitan's very sizable holdings of American art. This new installation by no means indicates an arrest in the growth of the collection, for there are still some relatively weak areas in which acquisitions will be made. On the other hand, never before have the strengths of the Museum's American arts been so splendidly displayed. Outstanding are the eighteenth-century portraits, Hudson River school landscapes, and notable examples of two of America's foremost painters—Winslow Homer and Thomas Eakins. The new sculpture court will give prominence to particularly fine examples of work by Hiram Powers and Augustus Saint-Gaudens. Noteworthy among the decorative arts are early furniture up to about 1820; baroque-style silver of about 1700, and the great presentation and exposition silver objects of the later nineteenth century; and nineteenth-century glass and ceramics, especially Pennsylvania German redware and Tiffany art glass.

Equally impressive are the range and variety of installation techniques, which include period rooms, permanent exhibition galleries, temporary exhibition galleries, and open study storage. Such diversity insures flexibility and the capacity for future growth and change in installation methods.

The Museum is fortunate to have secured one so able and well-qualified as Marshall B. Davidson to write this guide. Mr. Davidson, noted art critic and author, worked at the Museum for many years. He served as a curator in the American Wing and as editor of Museum publications, and no one is better qualified to give an overview of the Museum's American collections.

PHILIPPE DE MONTEBELLO
Director

INTRODUCTION

The collections of American art in the Metropolitan Museum are the most comprehensive and representative to be found anywhere. Here, under one roof, have been assembled significant examples in every medium and from all periods of this country's history, including acknowledged masterpieces in each of the many categories—painting, sculpture, architecture, prints and drawings, and decorative arts.

The first of such acquisitions were made almost immediately after the Museum was founded more than a century ago, and as the Museum grew in size and importance its holdings of American art increased in proportion. Before the middle of the present century these holdings had far outgrown the space and facilities available for exhibiting them coherently. Important new accessions could not be shown at all, or only in provisional and isolated settings.

About a decade ago ambitious plans were laid to correct this unsatisfactory situation by expanding the area devoted to American art and consolidating what had earlier perforce been displayed in different—sometimes widely separated—galleries. This was an undertaking of considerable magnitude; one that is only now beginning to reach fruition. Unfortunately, it also meant depriving the public of any substantial showing of American art while the new installations were being prepared. The original American Wing, which had opened with such great fanfare in 1924 and enjoyed a mounting popularity over the following half century, was closed. Its exhibits were put into storage while necessary changes were made in the arrangement of some of its rooms and galleries, and provisions were made for the accommodation of some better examples of interiors than those that had earlier been shown.

The exhibits in the original structure had mostly been limited to material dating before about 1825. Within the last several decades, the scope has been enlarged to include important examples of all kinds fashioned in the later years of the nineteenth century and the earlier years of the twentieth—years that witnessed achievements hardly less important to our cultural heritage than those of earlier times.

For all this, a large additional structure surrounding and adjacent to the old Wing was required. This has been undertaken by the architects Kevin Roche, John Dinkeloo & Associates of New Haven. As the present publication goes to press, construction is not altogether completed. In another year period rooms representing the various historical-revival styles of the later nineteenth century and a room from a house by Frank Lloyd Wright will be on view for the first time with appropriate furnishings. Other galleries then to be opened will show examples of Shaker craftsmanship and a selection of American folk art.

Nevertheless, a very considerable proportion of the collection is on permanent display at present, including some 25 period rooms and galleries, 300 of the finest paintings (with sculptures interspersed), and a larger number of individual objects of decorative art than has ever before been shown at one time. These displays of silver, pewter, glass, and ceramics further demonstrate the degrees of skilled craftsmanship that developed in response to the changing tastes of Americans over the centuries. Together with the newly designed garden court, with its numerous sculptures and flanking architectural elements by Louis Comfort Tiffany and Louis Sullivan, shown in the Museum for the first time, this array of native talent brings a fresh realization of the importance of our collections to an understanding of American art and of American experience.

M.B.D.

THE AMERICAN WING / *A GUIDE*

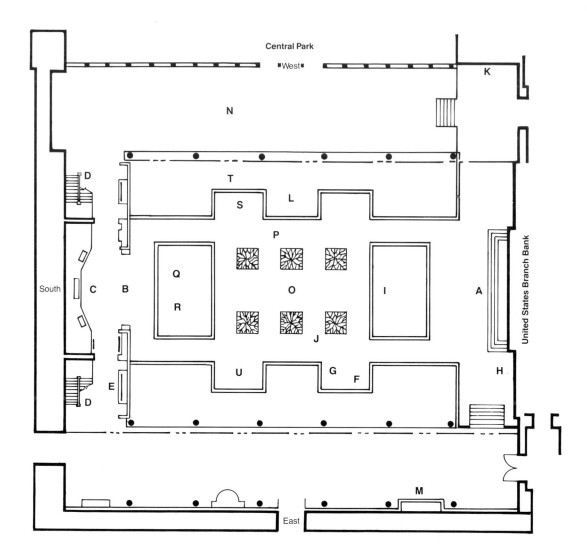

Locations of court sculptures and architectural elements

The letter of each object appears in the margin of the text where that object is discussed

A United States Branch Bank
B Tiffany loggia
C Tiffany wisteria window
D Sullivan staircases
E Wright window
F *California*
G *The White Captive*

H *Cleopatra*
I *The Babes in the Wood*
J *The Falling Gladiator*
K *William Cullen Bryant*
L *A Panther and Cubs*
M Vanderbilt mantelpiece
N *Struggle of the Two Natures in Man*

O *The Mares of Diomedes*
P *Bohemian Bear Trainer*
Q *Boy and Duck*
R *The Frog Fountain*
S *Dancer and Gazelles*
T *The Peacocks*
U *Mother and Child*

THE CHARLES ENGELHARD COURT

The ground-floor approach to the reconstituted American Wing leads from the main building into a spacious glass-roofed garden court, dedicated to Charles W. Engelhard. Landscaping of the court was designed by Umberto Innocenti and Richard K. Webel, and of the exterior grounds by Clara Coffee. A glass curtain continuous with the roof looks out to the west upon a view of Central Park. The architectural and sculptural displays that have been brought together in this lofty transparent enclosure are varied in style and mostly large in scale; they provide a dramatic introduction to the exhibits in adjoining areas.

At the northern end of the court rises the exterior façade of the old United States Branch Bank (cover), originally erected (A) on Wall Street in New York between 1822 and 1824. Built of marble from quarries at Tuckahoe, Westchester County, this neoclassic structure was designed by Martin F. Thompson, the architect of numerous other distinguished structures that have long since disappeared from lower Manhattan. When the bank was taken down in 1915, the old stones of the façade were carefully stowed away through the generous efforts of Robert W. de Forest, then president of the Museum. In 1924 they were reassembled in their present location.

A totally different architectural arrangement has been installed at the southern end of the court. Here, in brilliant contrast to the massive dignity of the bank façade, is the colorful loggia that once framed the main entrance of Laurelton Hall (FIG. 1). Designed by Louis Comfort Tiffany as his Oyster Bay, Long Island, residence, it was completed about 1905. At this time, Tiffany was America's most celebrated champion of the movement in design and decoration known as "art nouveau," and his work was as well known overseas as at home.

The exoticism and the use of sensuous color that characterize Tiffany's creations in various mediums are seen in the loggia. Islamic models inspired the well-traveled artist's use of two

pairs of columns and half-columns joined by stepped arches which are surmounted by a lintel faced with tiles of iridescent blue glass. The limestone columns themselves are topped with colorful ceramic capitals representing poppies in different stages of bloom. Within each of the three arches hangs a bell-shaped lantern of opalescent blue-and-gold glass. In 1918 Tiffany converted his estate into a retreat for artists, hoping that they would be inspired by the beauty of their surroundings.

Happily, the loggia survived a disastrous fire that swept Laurelton Hall in 1957. It was bought and removed from the site and presented to the Museum by Hugh and Jeannette McKean. Originally, the loggia led to glass doors opening into the house. In the present installation these have been replaced by a superb stained-glass window panel designed by Tiffany about 1905 for the New York residence of William Skinner (PL. 1). "The skill with which this glass is designed and executed," wrote one critic, "layered and tinted in subtle gradations to suggest distant mountains, sky, and water, is art and craft at its best." The view, a depiction of Oyster Bay framed by wisteria vines with clusters of luminous blue blossoms, recalls Tiffany's wisteria lamp shades. These were highly regarded about the turn of the century–and are still more so today. A superb mosaic column from Laurelton Hall and other products of Tiffany's peculiar genius are shown both here and elsewhere in the Wing.

The wisteria window is flanked by a pair of functioning metal staircases that were salvaged when the Chicago Stock Exchange Building was demolished in 1972 (FIG. 2). This doomed skyscraper, built in 1893-94, was one of the several architectural masterpieces designed by Louis H. Sullivan in association with the brilliant engineer Dankmar Adler. Sullivan, an almost exact contemporary of Tiffany, was an American prophet of modern architecture. As our exhibits demonstrate, he integrated utilitarian construction and handsome ornament with unique skill. Except for the white marble treads and mahogany handrails, the Museum's staircases are made of iron cast into attractive patterns and electroplated with bronze.

A selection of nineteenth- and early twentieth-century architectural elements installed on the landings midway up the staircases includes a cast-iron panel from the façade of a commercial building erected in lower Manhattan by James Bogardus in 1849. Bogardus was an outstanding pioneer in cast-iron

FIG. 1. (B)
View of the loggia, with ceramic capitals and glass tiles and lanterns, as it originally appeared at Laurelton Hall. Louis Comfort Tiffany (1848-1933) designed this Oyster Bay, Long Island, house for himself about 1905.

Gift of Jeanette Genius McKean and Hugh Ferguson McKean, in memory of Charles Hosmer Morse, 1978.10.1.

FIG. 2. (D)
Detail of one of two pairs of cast-iron staircases with electroplated bronze finish, designed by Louis H. Sullivan (1856-1924) for the Chicago Stock Exchange Building, 1893, shown here in situ before its removal to the museum.

Purchase, Mr. and Mrs. James Biddle Gift and Emily C. Chadbourne Bequest, 1972 (1972.50.1-4).

construction. Another decorative cast-iron panel, huge in scale, comes from the earliest building of any consequence designed by Sullivan, the Rothschild Building constructed about 1881 in Chicago's Loop.

Also shown is an ironwork grille that originally screened the banks of elevators in the Stock Exchange Building (FIG. 3). This is of special interest in that it is related to some of Frank Lloyd Wright's earliest ornamental work. It may indeed be his design, since he was a draftsman in Sullivan's office between 1887 and 1893. Sullivan's benign influence can be seen in a brightly glazed terra cotta block from the Farmer's and Mechanic's State Bank built in Hector, Minnesota, in 1916 by William G. Purcell and George Grant Elmslie. The latter had earlier worked for Sullivan and often drafted his intricate ornamental designs.

Nearby another window panel, conceived in 1911 for the playhouse of the children of Mr. and Mrs. Avery Coonley, presents a totally different innovation in color and design (PL. 2). Wright thought the Coonley residence at Riverside, Illinois, completed a few years earlier, was his best work up to that time. In this panel all references to natural themes have given way to abstract, geometric patterns, ultimately based on shapes from children's parties–balloons, flags, and confetti–expressed in primary colors. Its abstract design anticipates the nonobjective paintings of the avant-garde Dutch painter Mondrian. Wright called the triptych a "*Kinder*-symphony."

In the courtyard between the two architectural façades, a score or more of freestanding sculptures present a relatively brief but impressive introduction to the Museum's varied holdings in this field, and constitute a capsule history of the sculptor's art in America. Other examples, for the most part smaller in scale, can be seen in the galleries described in pages that follow. Those shown here are arranged in a roughly chronological and stylistic sequence running counterclockwise around the courtyard.

Sculpture began to flourish in America during the second quarter of the nineteenth century. Its ascendance was fostered by the wave of nationalism that followed the Revolution and the War of 1812, and by the young nation's vision of itself as the embodiment of the ideals of the republics of antiquity. The interest in the classical world was so widespread in America

PLATE 1. (C)
View of Oyster Bay, stained-glass wisteria window, made by Tiffany Studios (1900–1938)
for the house of William Skinner, 36 East Thirty-ninth Street, New York City, c. 1905.

From the McKean Collection through the courtesy of the Morse Gallery of Art, Winter Park, Florida.

PLATE 2. (E)
Stained-glass triptych window, designed by Frank Lloyd Wright
(1867-1959) for the Avery Coonley playhouse, Riverside, Illinois,
1912.

Purchase, The Edgar J. Kaufmann Charitable Foundation and Edward C. Moore Jr.
Gifts, 67.231.1-3.

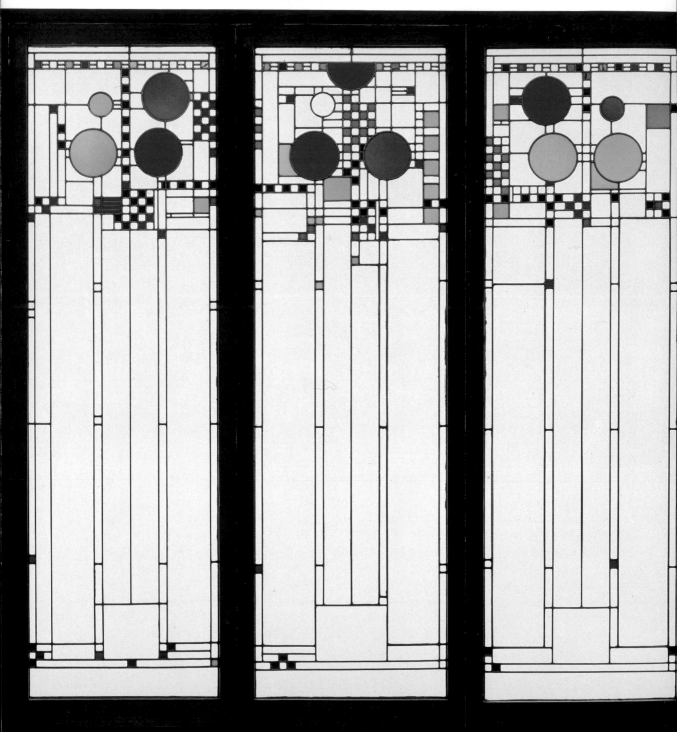

during this period that towns were named Athens, Rome, Troy, and Syracuse, and the neoclassical style dominated the arts and fashion. Sculpture executed in pure white marble became one of the most popular art forms because of its strong classical airs. Antique statuary was the major stylistic source for neoclassical sculptors, who draped their portraits in classical robes and based much of their ideal sculpture on subjects from classical mythology. Aspiring American artists traveled to Italy, the undisputed center of the neoclassical movement. There, rich collections of antique sculpture and a plentiful supply of pure white marble from the quarries of Carrara and Serravezza were readily available. There were, as well, many studio assistants capable of enlarging, carving, and finishing the sculptor's work.

The earliest neoclassical sculpture exhibited in the court-yard, a full-length nude figure, was designed in 1850 by the Vermont-born Hiram Powers as an allegorical representation of California. Powers spent most of his professional career in Florence, where he won an international reputation. *California* was the first sculpture by an American artist to be acquired by the Museum. *The White Captive* (FIG. 4), another graceful life-size nude of appropriately grave and chaste demeanor, was fashioned in a similar neoclassical spirit by Erastus Dow Palmer, a self-taught New Yorker who never went abroad for study. Palmer worked from live models, often one of his daughters. Although this was his first attempt at such a subject, possibly inspired by tales of the Indians' captives along the colonial frontier, it remains one of the finest of its kind made in America in the nineteenth century. It quickly won nationwide attention.

Thomas Crawford and William Wetmore Story, both of good family and with influential social and political connections, turned to sculpture as young men. Working largely in Rome, they earned enviable reputations in the years immediately preceding the Civil War. The literary allusions of both men's subjects added to their appeal to a contemporary public. Story's *Cleopatra* (FIG. 5) was praised by Nathaniel Hawthorne in *The Marble Faun*, published in 1861, and it was an instant success when it was first publicly shown the next year. Crawford's *The Babes in the Wood* (FIG. 6) illustrates verses from an old English nursery rhyme of the same title that was widely popular with

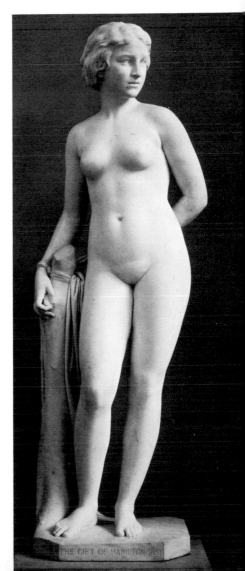

FIG. 4. (G)
The White Captive, by Erastus Dow Palmer (1817-1904), marble, 1858.
Bequest of Hamilton Fish, 1894 (94.9.3).

21

FIG. 5. (H)
Cleopatra, by William Wetmore
Story (1819-1895), marble,
1859; this version 1869.

Gift of John Taylor Johnston, 88.5.

FIG. 6. (I)
The Babes in the Wood, by
Thomas Crawford (c. 1813-
1857), marble, 1851.

Bequest of Hamilton Fish, 1894
(94.9.4).

Victorian sentimentalists. In his relatively short life, Crawford won numerous major public commissions in America, notably the colossal *Armed Freedom* atop the Capitol in Washington.

The Falling Gladiator (FIG. 7), standing in the west corridor of the courtyard, is one of the rare works by William Rimmer, a largely self-taught artist who was about forty-five years old and a practicing doctor before he began the serious pursuit of sculpture. When the original of this bronze was exhibited in Paris in 1862, the powerful realism of the anatomy, contrasting so remarkably with conventionally modeled figures of the day,

FIG. 7. (J)
The Falling Gladiator, by William Rimmer (1816-1879), bronze, 1861; this cast, 1907.
Rogers Fund, 07.224.

led to the unjust criticism that it was cast from life. Aside from this, Rimmer was neglected as an artist in his lifetime.

The Civil War drastically altered the social, economic, and cultural conditions of the nation. The country's rural society and agrarian economy were transformed into an urban society based upon an expanding industrialized economy. In the arts, the romanticism of the first half of the nineteenth century gave way to a new, more direct naturalism. Throughout the country and especially in the industrial North, there was an increasing desire to erect public statues to honor the nation's new political, civil, military, and industrial leaders. With this inundation of public monuments came a change from marble to bronze, a medium which could withstand exposure to the weather. Stylistically, post-Civil War naturalism evolved from neoclassical portraiture; however, the physical features of portraits of this period are no longer stylized or idealized, but realistically rendered. Sculptors now rarely cloaked their subjects in classical togas, but represented them instead in contemporary dress. Nonetheless, the compositions of most sculptures continued to be derived from classical sources, and it is this successful combining of classical composition and physically realistic portraiture that characterizes post-Civil War naturalism.

(K) The forthright naturalism of the era can be seen in a large bronze portrait bust of William Cullen Bryant, the famous poet and editor, created by Launt Thompson in 1867. After the Civil War, Edward Kemeys, a veteran of the Union Army, taught himself to model with the specific purpose of making (L) realistic likenesses of animals. *A Panther and Cubs* is typical of the work that led critics to consider him the only great American animal sculptor of his day.

During the last quarter of the nineteenth century, the United States experienced a period of unparalleled growth and extravagance. Rich railroad tycoons and the robber barons of industry made up a new ruling class. Generally they were men of little cultural background who spent lavishly on the arts, building enormous homes and commissioning large decorative paintings and sculptures. Paris became the new artistic center, and the Ecole des Beaux-Arts, the official French academy, the most important art school. The term "beaux-arts sculpture" is applied to works produced by these French-trained American artists. The style is characterized by an invigorated naturalism, richly textured surfaces, complex compositions, dramatic poses, the integration of the statue and its pedestal, and an increased emphasis on architectural works.

Among the first to turn from Rome to Paris was Augustus Saint-Gaudens, who returned to America in 1875 to become undisputed leader of the first generation of artists in the beaux-arts tradition. He was a towering figure in the American art world in general during the last decades of the nineteenth century and was showered with commissions and honors. In 1881-82, in collaboration with John La Farge, he fashioned the monumental marble and mosaic mantelpiece shown against the eastern wall of the court (FIG. 8). This was originally installed in

FIG. 8. (M)
Mantelpiece from the Vanderbilt house at Fifth Avenue and Fifty-seventh Street, marble, mosaic, and wood, by John LaFarge (1835-1910), George B. Post (1837-1913), and Augustus Saint-Gaudens (1848-1907), 1882.

Gift of Mrs. Cornelius Vanderbilt Sr., 25.234.

25

FIG. 10. (N) (OPPOSITE)
Struggle of the Two Natures in Man, by George Grey Barnard (1863-1938), marble, 1894.

Gift of Alfred Corning Clark, 96.11.

FIG. 9.
Mourning Victory: The Melvin Memorial, by Daniel Chester French (1850-1931), marble, 1908; this replica 1915.

Gift of James C. Melvin, 1912 (15.75).

the entrance hall of the Cornelius Vanderbilt residence at the corner of Fifth Avenue and Fifty-seventh Street, when that New York neighborhood was burgeoning with palatial homes of the very rich.

Saint-Gaudens's two heroic caryatids carved of numidian marble and representing Peace and Love support a lintel over which is framed a mosaic designed by La Farge. Above La Farge's central figure a Latin inscription reads, in translation, "The house at its threshold gives evidence of the master's good will. Welcome to the guest who arrives; farewell and helpfulness to him who departs."

The only contemporary American sculptor to approach Saint-Gaudens's fame was Daniel Chester French. His Melvin Memorial, commonly known as *Mourning Victory* (FIG. 9), is shown on the balcony level of the court. This is a marble copy of the 1909 original which marks the graves of three brothers of the Melvin family who died in the Civil War and were buried in Sleepy Hollow Cemetery, Concord, Massachusetts. French enjoyed a long and illustrious career. In 1874 he had executed the bronze statue of the *Minute Man*, also in Concord, which won him immediate fame; forty-eight years later he created the statue of Abraham Lincoln for that president's famous memorial at Washington.

Across the court in the west corridor *Struggle of the Two Natures in Man* (FIG. 10), a freestanding group cut in marble by George Grey Barnard, depicts the divine nature of man casting off his earthly self and reaching for the heavens. This dramatic work, with figures considerably larger than life-size, reveals Michelangelo's influence on Barnard. When it and a number of his other works were shown at the Paris Salon in 1894, French critics hailed the thirty-one-year-old American's special talent.

The dramatic tension displayed by Barnard's figures and the complicated poses that distinguish them from earlier neoclassical sculptures are found in the work of other sculptors who closed out the nineteenth century and opened the twentieth. *The Mares of Diomedes* (FIG. 11), a realistic and intensely dynamic bronze shown in the center courtyard, was completed in 1904 by Gutzon Borglum, best known for the enormous presidential portraits he carved on Mount Rushmore in South Dakota. The title of the piece alludes to the mythical man-eating horses of Diomedes, king of the Bistonians in Thrace, that were tamed

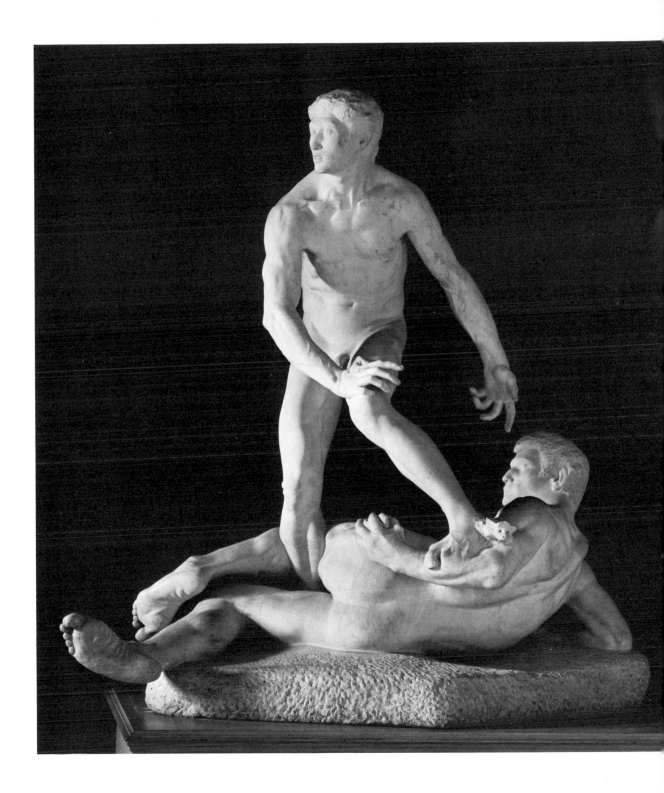

FIG. 11. (O)
The Mares of Diomedes, by Gutzon Borglum (1867-1941), bronze, 1904.

Gift of James Stillman, 06.1318.

FIG. 12. (Q)
Boy and Duck, by Frederick MacMonnies (1863-1937), bronze, 1898.

Rogers Fund, 22.61.

by Hercules as one of his twelve labors. However, these stampeding broncos more immediately suggest an episode of the American wild West, with a nude redskin performing a Herculean labor on the open prairie.

Bohemian Bear Tamer, by Paul Wayland Bartlett, is one of the best known works of this Connecticut Yankee, who lived most of his years in Paris. In 1889, when Bartlett was only twenty-four years old, this bronze was awarded a first prize by an international jury. Here again, the figure of an American Indian stands in for the nominal subject. Bartlett's equestrian statue of Lafayette, completed in 1907 and now to be seen in one of the courtyards of the Louvre, was so greatly admired that it was considered a fitting reciprocal offering to France for that nation's gift of the Statue of Liberty.

Boy and Duck (FIG. 12) is Frederick William MacMonnies's whimsical fountain group, installed in the central pool of the court. MacMonnies is another American artist who as a young man studied and lived in Paris, winning the high praise of French critics when he first showed his work there. Another

28

appropriately watery subject, *The Frog Fountain*, was made in Paris by Janet Scudder in 1901 when the Indiana-born artist was still in her twenties. It was the beginning of her successful career as a sculptor of fountains.

As the present century advanced the quite literal naturalism of the aforementioned groups gave way to a simplification of form that is compellingly illustrated by Paul Manship's highly stylized bronze group, *Dancer and Gazelles* (FIG. 13). The same spirit, with emphasis on linear pattern, is evident in *The Peacocks* (FIG. 14) by Manship's sometime assistant, Paris-born Gaston Lachaise.

The latest in this group of figural sculptures is *Mother and*

FIG. 13. (S)
Dancer and Gazelles, by Paul Manship (1885-1966), bronze, 1916.
Purchase, Francis Lathrop Bequest, 1959 (59.54).

FIG. 14. (T)

FIG. 14. (T)
The Peacocks, by Gaston
Lachaise (1882-1935), gilded
bronze, c. 1918; this cast 1922.
Gift of H. N. Slater, 50.173.

FIG. 15. (U)
Mother and Child, by William
Zorach (1889-1966), marble,
c. 1930.
Fletcher Fund, 52.143.

Child (FIG. 15), chiseled directly in marble between 1927 and
1930 by the Lithuanian-born sculptor William Zorach. The
freshly aroused interest in direct stone carving brought with it a
new emphasis on form and solidity that shows the influence of
cubism. However, the abstract quality of the resulting design
does not reduce the living expressiveness of the figures.

About the courtyard may be seen examples of cast-iron
furniture, popular for outdoor use in the nineteenth century.
Advances in iron founding and milling techniques made it
possible to fashion such forms in designs that followed all the
prevailing styles of the period.

THE BALCONY

Apart from the furniture and other objects shown in the period rooms and their adjoining galleries, the decorative arts in various mediums are abundantly displayed in the balcony overlooking the garden court. In these wide-ranging exhibits may be seen practically all the variations in design and craftsmanship that have marked the changing styles in American silver, pewter, glass, ceramics, and other materials over the last few hundred years.

Silver

Long before the Colonies produced a portrait painter or landscapist of any consequence, they supported scores of master craftsmen in the precious metals whose work was handsomely designed and scrupulously wrought. The silversmith, or goldsmith as he was often termed, was a banker of sorts, through whose skills the miscellaneous coins that flowed into America from different lands in the course of trade might be converted into handsome pieces of silver. The weight and purity of such plate was certified by the integrity of the smith who made and marked it, and it could be clearly identified by its owner in case of loss or theft, as coins could never be. It could also be put to practical use at table or be displayed as conspicuous wealth on a cupboard, and it could be easily reconverted into bullion or coin if need be.

Boston and New York (New Amsterdam) were the first New World centers of this highly practical art. As might be expected, work turned out in these two separate areas showed some marked regional differences in design. Among the earliest items exhibited here are several silver shillings and sixpences, coined at Boston by English-born John Hull and Robert Sanderson, by order of the General Court of Massachusetts in defiance of restrictions imposed by Britain against such practice. These pioneering smiths worked both in partnership and individually, turning out tankards, cups, and other forms that, except for the marks stamped on them, were indistinguishable from the relatively plain and serviceable objects produced in England at the time.

By the end of the seventeenth century baroque features associated with the William and Mary style found special expression in silverwork. The spool-shaped standing salt was made in Boston around the turn of the century by John Edwards and John Allen. A descendant of the great architectural salts that were a central feature of medieval and Renaissance dining boards, this example is ornamented with two bands of spiral gadrooning–that is, convex, or inverted, fluting. Similar bands distinguish a rare chocolate pot (FIG. 16) made in Boston by Edward Winslow about that same time, and an unusual sugar box made early in the eighteenth century by Daniel Greenough of New Castle, New Hampshire.

Both the salt and the box represent forms that had been held over from earlier English fashions and would soon be abandoned. The chocolate pot, on the other hand, is an early example of a form that had evolved in England only late in the seventeenth century, when drinking chocolate first became fashionable. Together with a triangular ink stand whose three feet were cast in the form of miniature lions, by John Coney, also of Boston, these few selected examples strongly remind us of the degree of affluence and the taste for luxury that had developed in New England less than a century after the settlement of that Puritan colony.

FIG. 16.
Silver chocolate pot, by Edward Winslow (1669-1753), Boston, 1700-1710.
Bequest of Alphonso T. Clearwater, 1933 (33.120.221).

FIG. 17.
Silver beaker, attributed to Jurian Blanck, Jr. (c. 1645-1714), New York City, c. 1683.
Joint property of The Reformed Protestant Dutch Church of Kingston, New York, and The Metropolitan Museum of Art, 33.120.621.

FIG. 18.

Pair of silver candlesticks and snuffer stand, by Cornelius Kierstede (1675-1757), New York City, 1700-1715.

Gift of Robert L. Cammann, 57.153ab; Gift of Mrs. Clermont L. Barnwell, 64.83ab; Gift of Mr. and Mrs. William A. Moore, 23.80.21.

The silver fashioned in New York in the late seventeenth century and the early eighteenth reflects the mingling of Dutch, English, and French traditions. A beaker made about 1683 by Jurian Blanck, Jr. (FIG. 17), with engraved figures of Faith, Hope, and Charity and a Dutch inscription, represents a type of vessel used both for domestic and sacramental purposes. A silver teakettle with a grotesque spout by Cornelius Kierstede, and a small handsomely decorated globular teapot by Jacob Boelen, are the earliest known American examples of these forms. They were made at a time when tea, like coffee, was still a rare, exotic, and expensive novelty.

Kierstede, probably the most individualistic of early American craftsmen, also fashioned a boldly embossed six-paneled bowl whose design is peculiar to New York, and a unique pair of stop-fluted candlesticks (FIG. 18). These, with a matching

33

FIG. 19.
Silver teapot, by Peter Van Dyck (1684-1751), New York City, 1715-1725.
Rogers Fund, 47.7.

snuffer stand, have splayed bases chased with fantastic designs of vaguely oriental character. This inventive decoration owed much to Dutch design. Silver tankards made in New York early in the eighteenth century were capacious, flat topped, and broad based. This example by Simeon Soumaine with flat engraved lid, corkscrew-shaped thumbpiece, little cast masks and garland applied to the handle, and ornamental base molding, displays a combination of decorative features peculiar to New York.

The suave simplicity of the succeeding Queen Anne style is handsomely demonstrated in a pear-shaped teapot (FIG. 19). It was fashioned by Peter Van Dyck of New York about 1715-25 for Myndert Schuyler, twice mayor of Albany. As the ritual of drinking tea developed, new forms evolved for serving the beverage—sugar bowls and tongs, milk and cream pitchers, teaspoons, tea caddies, and other novelties, as displayed in this gallery. The sober restraint of Queen Anne design may be seen here in a variety of other forms as well, notably in a pair of trimly modeled candlesticks by Edward Winslow and a capacious two-handled cup by Jacob Hurd, both Boston smiths.

With the gradual emergence of the rococo style in the middle years of the eighteenth century, greater elaboration of form and decoration once again became the fashion. The rococo influence that spread from France to England and America can be seen in a snuffer tray with cast and chased scroll and shell ornaments by Philip Syng, Jr. of Philadelphia. A pair of salts with cast dolphin feet and floral appliques, by Charles Le Roux, epitomize the Huguenot contribution to silvermaking as it was practiced in the Hudson River Valley.

There were Huguenot craftsmen in Boston and Philadelphia as well. Apollos Rivoire, a smith who came from France by way of Guernsey Island, Americanized his name to Paul Revere after he arrived at Boston, and had a son and namesake whose silverwork is well represented in our collections. On display among other examples by this celebrated patriot are a tankard with a domed lid, one of a pair of canns, or mugs, and a handsomely shaped three-legged sauceboat.

The sauceboat represents one of the variety of new forms for domestic use that evolved with the rococo style. A case in point

FIG. 20.
Silver cake basket, by Myer Myers (1723-1795), New York City, 1760-1770.

Morris K. Jesup Fund, 54.167.

is the rare, intricately pierced cake basket by Myer Myers of
New York (FIG. 20), a Jewish silversmith of Dutch descent.
Undulating curved outlines, delicate and variegated cutout
patterns, and shells on the rim give this piece an airy elegance
that characterizes the rococo spirit. (Myers produced a variety
of other forms for colonial synagogues, and still others for
Protestant churches.) That same spirit is expressed in more
solid form in a pair of candlesticks by the same maker and by a
sugar bowl of inverted pear shape with raised and chased foliate
decoration. The latter was probably made by Jacob Boelen II,
also a New York smith of Dutch descent.

One of the most engaging examples of precious metalwork in
this lively style is a very rare child's coral and bells or rattle (FIG.
21). An ornately fashioned hollow gold stem decorated with two
rows of bells terminates at one end in a whistle and at the other
in a handle of coral, a substance that from ancient times was
considered to have medicinal and magical properties. The rattle
was made by Nicholas Roosevelt, still another New York
craftsman of Dutch descent.

In the rococo period tea sets were occasionally designed en
suite, with teapot, creamer, sugar bowl, and other accessories
designed as related elements. This practice became commonplace with the introduction of classic-revival styles in the
years following the Revolution. Outstanding among the numerous examples on display is a four-piece tea service attributed to Philadelphia silversmith Christian Wiltberger. This
group is said to have been given by George Washington to his
adopted daughter Eleanor (Nellie) Custis on the occasion of her
marriage to Lawrence Lewis in 1799. The set is an impressive example of the Federal, or neoclassical, style in silver with
its urn and helmet shapes, its shallow alternating convex and
concave panels with bright-cut engraved designs, and its patriotic eagle finials. A large vase-shaped tea urn, also in the Federal
style, once again bears Revere's mark. Its restrained design
contrasts sharply with the vigorous shapes of many other pieces
by this versatile craftsman.

The neoclassical mode is directly and simply expressed in a
pair of candlesticks in the form of fluted columns fashioned by
Isaac Hutton of Albany, New York (FIG. 22). Strong French
influence is apparent in a pair of elaborate sauceboats made in

Philadelphia by the émigré smith Anthony Rasch (FIG. 23). The sinuous serpents that serve as handles, the ram's-head spouts, and the winged-lion feet are ornamental forms derived from classical antiquity. Thus, too, the animal-head spouts of a punch pot made by Simon Chaudron, a onetime partner of Rasch and also a French-born Philadelphian, resemble decorations derived from ancient models that were popular during Napoleon's Empire. As the influence of French Empire and English Regency styles increased, more robust versions of classical design were introduced. Among other examples, this may be seen in a coffee pot by Garrett Eoff of New York, with heavy flutes and prominent paw feet.

The later years of the nineteenth century witnessed the revival of a number of other historic styles. These interpretations of the past were so free that they amounted to a new vocabulary of design, telling more about their own time than about the taste of earlier times. Changing styles in furniture and silver were closely related—styles that resulted in a bewildering mixture of forms and decoration. The labels given to these

FIG. 22.
Pair of silver candlesticks, by Issac Hutton (1766-1855), Albany, New York, 1800-1815.
Bequest of Alphonso T. Clearwater, 33.120.204-05.

PLATE 4. (OPPOSITE)
"Adams" vase, gold, pearls, and semiprecious stones, designed by Paulding Farnham and made by Tiffany and Company for presentation to Edward Dean Adams, Chairman of the board of American Cotton Oil Company, 1893-1895.
Gift of Edward D. Adams, 04.1.

FIG. 23.
One of a pair of silver sauceboats, by Anthony Rasch (c. 1778-1859?), Philadelphia, c. 1815-1820.
Sansbury-Mills Fund, 59.152.1.

FIG. 24.
Silver hot-water kettle, by Ball,
Tompkins & Black, New York
City, 1850.
Gift of Mrs. F. R. Lefferts, 69.141.a-c.

successive, overlapping styles—Gothic, rococo, and Renaissance among them—provided only a vague guide to their appearance.

By mid-century the late neoclassical American Empire style had largely been replaced by what were called rococo and Renaissance patterns. Characteristically, hollow ware was almost completely covered with heavy chased C- and S-scrolls and diapers combined with bold repoussé ornament in naturalistic floral designs. Two tea services produced by the prominent New York firm of Ball, Tompkins, and Black are fine, highly typical examples of these lushly ornamental fashions (FIG. 24).

In 1874, to honor William Cullen Bryant on the occasion of his eightieth birthday, a group of the poet's friends commissioned James H. Whitehouse of Tiffany and Company to fashion the huge vase shown in this gallery. Although this massive piece has the outlines of an antique Greek vase, it is overlaid with complex ornamentation that includes a profile portrait of Bryant, symbolic representations of American flora and fauna, and Renaissance-revival medallions referring to the poet's writings and interests. Bryant gave the vase to the Museum a few years after it had been presented to him.

In their opulence, symbolism, and eclecticism, two other large and impressive vases made by Tiffany and Company represent the extravagant taste of America's Gilded Age. The complexity of design of both the so-called Magnolia vase and the Adams vase (PLS. 3, 4) is practically indescribable, calling for expert craftsmanship of a kind that could probably not be commanded today. A ewer and basin made early in the present century by the Gorham Manufacturing Company of Providence, Rhode Island, were fashioned in the art nouveau style. Such Martelé wares were made of purer and softer metal than sterling silver. The plain surfaces of the basin and ewer reveal the marks left in the soft metal as each piece was hammered by hand to its unique shape. Here, as in an elegant paper knife by Unger Brothers of Newark, New Jersey, are the freely flowing organic forms and ornaments typical of the art nouveau style. It appeared to many that the modern world had finally cast off the bonds of the past, exuberantly turned away from historical precedent, and confidently restated the principles of design in purely contemporary terms. More recently this shift has been viewed as part of a continuing cycle in which straight-line and curvilinear styles alternate.

Pewter

Throughout the colonial and early Federal periods pewter, made principally of tin with small admixtures of lead and antimony, was a ubiquitous metal, serving myriad human wants from the nursery to the banquet hall, from the tavern to the Communion table. It is a relatively soft and destructible alloy, but it may be easily melted and remolded at small expense. The brass molds in which pewter was cast, however, were costly to make and replace, and their prolonged use tended to retard developments in design. Thus, since forms in pewter were often modeled after those hammered in silver, the styles of pewter porringers, tankards, teapots, and other vessels persisted long after silversmiths had abandoned them for more fashionable ones.

The Museum owns a particularly fine collection of pewter (FIG. 25). Although forms are more or less standardized because of the reliance on molds, the lasting attraction of this metalwork may be judged by the number of outstanding examples on display. An eighteenth-century porringer by one Francis Bassett (either father, or son and namesake) of New York, has a pierced handle remarkably similar in design to those found on English models and identical with those found on porringers by some other early American pewterers.

Probably just before the Revolutionary War, John Will, another New York pewterer, made a tankard whose form was typical but whose ornament—engraved floral designs on body and domed lid—were unusual. To make such a piece of hollow ware, as many as four molds were required: one each for the body, the lid, the thumbpiece for opening the lid, and the handle. Will's slightly earlier contemporary Simon Edgell of Philadelphia fashioned a magnificent fifteen-inch dish of excellent metal strengthened by scrupulous allover hammering. In addition to these prime examples are an inverted pear-shaped teapot standing on little cabriole legs with claw-and-ball feet, by William Will; a unique christening basin by Joseph Leddel; a mug by Frederick Bassett; and a tall flagon by Johann Christoph Heyne—all typifying what is best and most significant in eighteenth-century American pewter.

FIG. 25.
Pewter chalice, by Johann Christoph Heyne (1715-1781), Lancaster, Pennsylvania, c. 1756-1780.

Gift of Joseph France, 43.162.29.

Early in the nineteenth century, a finer grade of pewter known as britannia was introduced into this country. This silver-white alloy contained no lead but some copper to give the metal hardness and more antimony to give it a bright sheen. Because it was a tough alloy that could be rolled into thin sheets, then spun into the desired shape on a lathe or stamped into the needed component parts by a press, britannia lent itself to a host of diversified objects. From the 1830s to the 1860s this adaptable metal was at the height of its popularity.

Thomas Danforth Boardman of Hartford, Connecticut, one of a number of related pewterers with the same surname, was among the first Americans to produce britannia ware. A large two-quart flagon and a two-handled beaker are examples of the work he produced in partnership with Sherman Boardman in the second quarter of the century. The enormous variety of forms manufactured in quantities during britannia's heyday—everything from cuspidors to Communion services, from candlesticks and lamps to picture frames and babies' bottles, from teapots and spoons to earpieces for hearing trumpets and signal lamps—can hardly be suggested by the selected pieces here displayed; but the quality of performance at its best clearly survived the industrialization of this ancient craft.

Glass

Of the many materials used in the decorative arts glass lends itself to the greatest variety of treatment. It can be freely blown and tooled to any conceivable form; it can be fashioned into a film of gossamer thinness or a solid of weighty bulk; it can be blown or pressed into patterned molds of many different shapes; it can be cut and engraved in glittering textures; it can be given gemlike colors that range the spectrum or endowed with crystalline clarity; it can be enameled with colorful designs. Over the past two centuries American glassmakers have taken advantage of all these possibilities to produce such examples from the Museum's collections as are here on display.

Glassmakers were included among the earliest immigrants, from Jamestown on, but the craft achieved a significant output only when the eighteenth century was well advanced and when artisans, Germans for the most part, established furnaces in several different colonies. Among the more enduring of these was the factory established by Caspar Wistar near Alloway in

FIG. 26.
Glass pocket flask, probably
made at the American Flint
Glass Manufactory (1765-1774)
established by Henry William
Stiegel, Manheim, Pennsylvania, 1764-1774.

Gift of Frederick W. Hunter, 14.74.17.

southern New Jersey in 1739, with the aid of craftsmen brought
to America from the Continent. German influence is clearly
evident in the glassware produced by this factory, which oper-
ated for nearly forty years. Here, as at most American glasshouses until well into the nineteenth century, the commercial
product consisted primarily of green bottles and window
panes. Wistar, however, also produced tablewares of both green
("common") and colorless glass. Several sugar bowls, taper-
sticks, and other articles have been attributed to the Wistar-
burgh factory.

During the dozen years before the Revolution the Pennsylvania glasshouses of the fabulous "Baron" Henry William
Stiegel, another German entrepreneur, advertised products as
good as any imported from abroad. The pattern-molded sugar
bowls, creamers, salts, syllabub and jelly glasses, and other
forms often attributed to Stiegel's several furnaces (FIG. 26)
were in fact expertly made of good metal (the technical word for
molten glass). For the most part these attractive bright-colored
pieces are indistinguishable from others known to have been
made abroad.

Among the finest fully identified surviving pieces of eighteenth-century American glass are two handsomely engraved
presentation goblets made in the New Bremen, Maryland,
factory of John Frederick Amelung. The first, dated 1788, was
very likely presented by Amelung to his German financial
backers to prove his success with his New World glass factory
(FIG. 27). The other goblet, engraved with the arms of the state
of Pennsylvania, was presented by Amelung to Thomas Mifflin
when he became governor of that state in 1791.

Amelung had arrived in America from Bremen, Germany, in
1784. He was accompanied by about sixty experienced work-
men and armed with letters of recommendation from John
Adams and Benjamin Franklin, both of whom were then in
Europe. His enterprise soon won the notice of George Washington. Despite these advantages, his venture collapsed in 1795
and Amelung's craftsmen moved on to factories elsewhere in
the new nation. Glassblowers were peripatetic craftsmen any-
way, and the influence of these eary artisans is probably to be
seen in glass made later in New York, New England, Pennsylvania, Ohio, and elsewhere whither they and their descendants
migrated from those pioneering factories.

FIG. 27.
Covered glass goblet, made at
the New Bremen Glass Man-
ufactory (1787-1795) established
by John Frederick Amelung,
New Bremen, Maryland, 1788.

Rogers Fund, 28.52a,b.

Throughout the colonial and early Federal periods, no American product could compete with the fine, clear glass imported from overseas. The first venture to do so successfully was launched in 1808 when Benjamin Bakewell established a glasshouse at Pittsburgh which produced clear lead glass, deeply and brilliantly cut in the English fashion. At the time, it was said, New Yorkers supposed Pittsburgh "to be at the farther end of the world." The development of a successful and sophisticated glasshouse in Pittsburgh was therefore surprising, and was an early indication of the booming economic potential of the American Midwest. A few years later President James Monroe ordered from Bakewell a large service engraved with the arms of the United States for the White House.

Typical of the workmanship of Pittsburgh's craftsmen in the 1820s is a decanter embellished with a cut strawberry-and-diamond pattern in the manner of contemporary English and Irish designs. A tumbler of clear, heavy glass which has cut decoration and a ceramic cameo portrait of Lafayette embedded in the base was made at the Bakewell plant in 1825 to commemorate the French veteran's return visit to America.

In 1818, ten years after the Bakewell plant opened, Deming Jarvis of the New England Glass Company undertook similar productions in cut glass, continuing them at the Boston and Sandwich Glass Company which he founded in 1825. At this time, other successful furnaces that produced fine wares were operating at Pittsburgh and elsewhere in Pennsylvania, New England, New York, and New Jersey.

At numerous factories, designs very roughly approximating those of cut glass were produced by blowing a gather of glass into full-size patterned molds hinged in three or four sections. The result was a relatively inexpensive tableware now commonly referred to as "three-mold" or "blown-three-mold" glass. The practice was an ancient one, although American craftsmen did not know of the precedents. This method could not duplicate the sharp facets of cut glass, but it produced engaging objects exemplified by several decanters and other forms in the balcony displays. Patterns cut into the molds were not always so sharply geometrical as those of the glass cutter, but branched out into baroque and other more freely flowing styles.

Another technique commonly practiced in nineteenth-century America involved the use of small, open pattern molds into which a gather of molten glass was inserted, then withdrawn and blown into whatever larger shape was desired. The subtly graduated moldings formed by the expansion of the design impressed on the original gather of glass, greater in one area than another (as in the figures on a toy balloon as it is blown up) resulted in surfaces that in changing light take on the effect of rippling movement. The technique (also ancient in origin) is associated with Stiegel's pre-Revolutionary operation. A flask thus produced in amethyst-colored glass and impressed with what is known as a diamond-daisy pattern may well have been a Stiegel product. Years later the technique was employed at factories in the Midwest. A flask of light blue glass, an amber compote, bottle, and sugar bowl, all made in the Ohio area in the 1830s and '40s, exemplify the flowering of this ages-old method in the American Midwest.

Other types of molds, hinged in two sections, were used to produce patterned whiskey flasks and bottles. The molded designs often celebrated some important occasion or prominent public figure, providing an informal pictorial commentary on the passing national scene during the years from the War of 1812 to the Civil War. Craftsmen at the factories that turned out these and other inexpensive commonplace products, including window glass, in commerical quantities, also produced tablewares of some distinction. Using the same unrefined glass, they produced objects for their own purposes and for sale to local customers. A pair of exceptionally handsome blue-green candlesticks (FIG. 28) and a light green pitcher and bowl, both overlaid with decorative loops or "lily pads," are presumably pieces of this sort. These forms are in the traditional vernacular of the glassblower freely manipulating his material with age-old techniques.

The first important change in the fashioning of glass since the pre-Christian era was the development of the method of mechanically pressing glass into patterned molds. This technique enabled various forms with intricate designs to be mass manufactured in exact duplicates quickly and at moderate cost. Deming Jarvis introduced the process in the early nineteenth century at the Boston and Sandwich Glass Company, and it was soon put to use in a number of other glasshouses both east

47

FIG. 28.
Pair of glass candlesticks, southern New Jersey, 1825-1850.

Rogers Fund, 35.124.1,2.

and west of the Allegheny Mountains (FIG. 29). Although the mechanically pressed ware was first meant to imitate cut glass, the iron-and-brass molds into which the molten glass was forced could be modeled with more precise, minute detail than a glass cutter's wheel could achieve. Backgrounds of delicate stippling that caught, reflected, and refracted any light that played against them gave this so-called "lacy" glass a novel and distinctive character. It found a large appreciative audience from the beginning—and it still does among collectors. As in the case of three-mold glass, in the 1830s and '40s designers of pressed-glass molds departed from geometrical cut-glass prototypes and combined rococo, Gothic, and classical motifs with patriotic symbols in highly original combinations.

The pressing process also made it feasible to produce forms of a sort no glassblower could duplicate. This possibility, clearly demonstrated in a variety of novel lacy-glass shapes, became even more manifest in the 1860s and '70s when a number of glasshouses converted to the manufacture of pressed glassware of cheaper metal. By then, improved pressing techniques made possible a still wider variety of designs and forms and the trend toward producing glassware in complete table settings was

FIG. 29.

Pressed glass bowl, probably New England, 1830-1835.

Gift of Mrs. Charles W. Green, in memory of Dr. Charles W. Green, 51.171.153.

FIG. 30.

Glass compote, probably made by Bakewell, Pears & Company (1836-1882), Pittsburgh, Pennsylvania, 1860-1870.

Gift of Mrs. Emily Winthrop Miles, 46.140.83ab.

established. This so-called "pattern glass," given such suggestive trade names as Westward Ho, Ashburton, Lincoln Drape, and so on, made attractive tableware available to a large public at low prices. The lower quality of the glass used was sometimes camouflaged by partly frosting the surfaces and by other devices. A compote on display, for example, is pressed in what was known as the Thumbprint pattern (FIG. 30), an allover design of oval facets whose highly reflective surfaces, while simulating the effect of good cut glass, tend at the same time to disguise any imperfections in the metal used. Popular favorites from about the 1840s to the 1870s were figural subjects in the round, such as the candlesticks in the shape of dolphins. Another classical motif is represented by a candlestick pressed in the likeness of a caryatid, a design patented by the New England Glass Company in 1870 and produced with variations at other factories.

During the middle decades of the nineteenth century, free-blown glass of fine quality continued to be made in quantity. Cases in point are a handsome clear-glass pitcher decorated with applied threading and mid bands and with an English shilling of 1827 in the hollow knop of its stem. It was probably

FIG. 31.
Cut and engraved glass compote, made at the Greenpoint Glassworks (1852-1863) established by Christian Dorflinger, Brooklyn, New York, c. 1861.

Gift of Kathryn Hait Dorflinger Manchee, 1972.232.1.

made by the New England Glass Company. A bank, also of clear glass and possibly a product of the Sandwich factory, has a "bird" finial and five- and ten-cent United States coins in the hollow knops beneath the finial and at the base respectively. An exceptionally fine compote (FIG. 31) engraved with a version of the United States seal and a band of decorative motifs was made about 1861 at the Greenpoint Glass Works in Brooklyn, New York, by Christian Dorflinger, a French émigré who at this time was supplying tableware for the White House on order of Mrs. Lincoln.

Throughout the last half of the nineteenth century a wide variety of innovations in glassmaking succeeded one another as popular fashions. Encasing loopings of colored glass in clear metal was one technique that showed off the craftsmanship of the blower and resulted in attractive and lively products. A pair of vases with globular covers known as "witch balls," probably made at the New England Glass Company, are laced with swirling loops of red, white, and blue glass (FIG. 32).

An outstanding technical achievement perfected during these years was that of coating clear glass forms with thin layers of colored glass, then cutting through the latter to leave a pattern in the clear glass beneath that was sometimes engraved. This technique, copied from wares produced in Bohemia, is brilliantly represented here in a ruby-colored decanter made at the Sandwich factory in 1867. In an earlier example, a lamp base possibly made at the same factory, an opaque white overlay is cut away in attractive patterns to expose the ruby glass underneath. Expert craftsmen recently immigrated from Germany and France contributed importantly to such developments.

In the last quarter of the century a great demand for "artistic glass" encouraged glassmakers to make even greater efforts to produce an almost bewildering abundance of richly colored and textured and fancifully shaped wares. It was a period of constant invention and innovation that brought forth many-colored and variously-ornamented forms. These were patented at different factories under such suggestive trade names as Burmese, Peachblow, Pomona, Amberina, and Agate–appealing to the

FIG. 32.

Glass urns with witch balls, probably New England Glass Company (1818-1888), East Cambridge, Massachusetts, 1850-1875.

Purchase, The Edgar J. Kaufmann Foundation Gift, 69.84.lrab,2rab.

contemporary taste for the exotic in all sorts of household furnishings. Various examples of these popular but short-lived fashions indicate the high degree of virtuosity that contributed to the success of these styles.

The last years of the century also saw the development of cut glass on an unprecedented scale. During this so-called "brilliant period," the glass was made of heavy, lustrous metal precisely cut from any one of innumerable patterns with as many different names. Housewives were reminded that such glassware constituted the "most showy, and, in many respects, choicest of table equipments." Another fashion of the period was glass on which a pattern in a thin silver coating was deposited, then further defined by engraved or etched details. The swirling overlays of a vase so ornamented with a design of willowy tulips and interlaced leaves handsomely expresses the spirit of art nouveau.

By far the most influential innovator of these years, and an active proponent of the art nouveau movement, was Louis Comfort Tiffany, whose genius and international reputation have already been briefly referred to in the discussion of the Garden Court. It has been estimated that by 1898 Tiffany had created five thousand colors and varieties of his famous Favrile glass (PL. 6), which was hailed by *The House Beautiful* as "a distinctively American product that is recognized wherever it is shown as an achievement in art." The report went on to observe that Tiffany's Favrile vases had "all the splendor of opals, emeralds, aquamarines, and chrysoprus . . . colors stolen from hyacinths, tulips, and roses, from garnets, corals, and turquoise. Iridescence . . . [is] irradiated with purple and gold." That statement, published some eighty years ago, can stand as a summary description of the numerous examples of vases, lamps, and other forms from the Museum's collections on exhibition here.

Ceramics

Clays that could be used for making various types of pottery were plentiful in colonial America, as of course was wood to fire the potters' kilns. As a result, ceramics were made to serve local needs in various colonies from the earliest days of settlement. Then and for many years to come, not only bricks but roof tiles and kitchen, dairy, and table equipment were made of coarse red earthenware—simple, utilitarian forms that were usually washed or splashed with protective and sometimes decorative glazes of various colors.

These practical wares were made in many places, with some regional differences in form and style of decoration. Outstanding was the highly distinctive pottery of the Pennsylvania Germans, with colorful, sprightly designs and inscriptions. A wide variety of forms from pitchers, jugs, plates, and mugs to flowerpots, shaving basins, and toy whistles were made. Two basic techniques were employed in the application of these designs: slip decoration and sgraffito. Both methods were centuries old and both were practiced in other areas of the country. Slip decoration was achieved by drawing colored liquid clay, or "slip," on the pottery with a goose quill before the final firing. Sgraffito designs were scratched through a slip coating with a stick, revealing the red clay base beneath (PL. 5). Graphic motifs and inscriptions were commonly taken from folk images and folklore carried over from the Old World to the New.

Stoneware, made of finer and denser clays that were fired at a much higher temperature than ordinary earthenware, was produced as early as the eighteenth century. The harder body of this ware could be glazed merely by throwing salt into the kiln when the fire was at its hottest, thus coating the object with a thin, colorless, very hard film that was impervious to liquids. It was also resistant to acids, so that salt-glazed stoneware was popular for containers for vinegar, pickles, preserves, and the like. The practical advantages of such a ware were obvious and it was produced in various regions of the country throughout the nineteenth century.

Most stoneware was gray in color with decoration painted freehand in cobalt blue. One jug on exhibit bears the incised inscription "Iohn Havins, 1775, July 18, N. York" and the mark I. C., probably the initials of the potter John Crolius of New York City (FIG. 33). A cistern made about a century later in Strasburg, Virginia—a more elaborate form with dolphin-shaped handles, a child's bust for a finial, and other applied decorations—illustrates the enduring popularity of stoneware.

One of the most extensively produced types of pottery from abut 1830 was a more pretentious earthenware which was mottled or streaked with a lustrous brown glaze often resembling tortoiseshell. It was known as Rockingham because pot-

FIG. 33.
Stoneware jug, probably made by John Crolius (1733-1812), New York City, c. 1775.

Rogers Fund, 34.149.

tery so glazed was first made in the eighteenth century at Swinton, England, on the estate of the Marquis of Rockingham. This and some other new types of pottery were shaped in molds rather than thrown on the wheel. This technique, like that of pressing glass, shifted the emphasis from the craftsman to the designer of molds, and opened the door to mass production. Rockingham was molded to create a wide variety of forms: doorknobs, paperweights, cuspidors, picture frames, pudding bowls, lamp bases, pitchers, and decorative objects of different sorts. It was produced at a number of factories in New Jersey, Maryland, Vermont, and Ohio. Representative examples are the figure of a reclining doe before a hollow tree trunk, attributed to designer Daniel Greatbach at Bennington, Vermont, in the 1850s; and a hound-handled pitcher produced at East Liverpool, Ohio, about 1847, a favored design with an English prototype that was made with variations at a number of potteries.

Short-lived attempts to produce true porcelain were undertaken as early as the eighteenth century, notably from 1771 to 1772 by Bonnin and Morris of Philadelphia. A rare few of their works have survived. But it was in 1825 that William Ellis Tucker, also of Philadelphia, opened the first really successful porcelain factory to operate in America. The enterprise lasted only until 1838 but in that brief time produced thin, white, translucent wares that competed with European imports.

Although, with the help of immigrant French craftsmen and some backing from local associates, Tucker (in partnership at various times with either Thomas Hulme or Judge Joseph Hemphill) turned out some elaborate pieces, most of the firm's output consisted of relatively simple adaptations of fashionable French, German, and English designs. Among them are the monogrammed coffee service made for a member of the Tucker family, part of which is on display, and several pitchers painted with imaginery landscapes in sepia and polychrome and with floral decorations in natural colors (FIG. 34). The shapes of these pieces reflect the neoclassical spirit of the time.

Parian ware, a white, waxy porcelain developed in England for use in unglazed objects, was introduced into this country around the middle of the last century. It was so named because of its resemblance to marble quarried on the Aegean island of Paros. Indeed, it proved a happy substitute for that stone when

FIG. 34.
Porcelain pitcher, made at the American China Manufactory (1826-1838), established by William Ellis Tucker, Philadelphia, 1826-1838.
Purchase, Mrs. Russell Sage Gift, 1970.112.

it was molded into statuettes which were sometimes described as having been made of Parian marble. A case in point is the bust of Ulysses S. Grant, modeled by W. H. Edge at James Carr's New York City Pottery for display at the Philadelphia Centennial exhibition of 1876. There is also a sculptural quality to a Niagara Falls pitcher made by the United States Pottery Company at Bennington, Vermont, in celebration of America's natural wonders. Unlikely as such a subject was, the resultant form, an extreme expression of the naturalistic rococo decoration favored at the time, was surprisingly effective. Color was often used in Parian ware: a smooth white design stands out in relief against a pitted ground of blue, pink, buff, or green. These pieces were finished by hand.

The United States International Exhibition, known as the Centennial, provided an excellent showcase for the improved porcelains that had been developed since mid-century. The Union Porcelain Works of Greenpoint (Brooklyn), New York, showed its Century Vase, designed for the occasion by the gifted German-born sculptor Karl Mueller. A version of this monumental piece (the original was reportedly over seven feet in height) displays a relief profile of George Washington and has buffalo heads for handles. Panels in a band around the base contain relief figures recalling various aspects of American history. Mueller was also responsible for an impressive pedestal of biscuit (unglazed) porcelain with neoclassical figures in white relief against an apricot-colored ground (FIG. 35). Like the pedestal, the so-called Liberty Cup, shown at the exhibition by the Union Porcelain Works brings to mind the designs of classical subjects introduced by the celebrated English potter Josiah Wedgwood in the late eighteenth century.

American ceramics came into their own in the years following the Centennial. For the first time the products of American kilns were winning international recognition for their technical quality and artistic interest. As in the case of American glass during the same years, design in ceramics was affected by a craving for what a contemporary referred to as "civilizing, refining, and elevating" *objets d'art*. The most distinctive achievements were those of the artist-potters whose commercial output reflected the principles and ideals of the current English Arts and Crafts movement. In other words, the esthetic qualities of the objects were in accord with their utilitarian

PLATE 6. (OPPOSITE)
Favrile glass bottle and vases by Louis Comfort Tiffany, Corona, New York, 1892-1928.
Gift of H. O. Havemeyer, 96.17.46; Gift of Louis Comfort Tiffany Foundation, 51.121.17; Anonymous Gift 55.213.12, 27.

FIG. 35.
Porcelain pedestal, Union Porcelain Works (1863-c. 1920), Greenpoint, Brooklyn, New York, c. 1876.
Purchase, Anonymous Gift, 68.99.1a-d.

Ceramics

FIG. 36.
Earthenware vase, Grueby
Faience Company (1894-1911),
Boston, 1899-1910.

Purchase, The Edgar J. Kaufmann
Foundation Gift, 69.91.2.

forms. The Arts and Crafts philosophy was that art in the broadest sense could and should be part of everyday life.

It was in keeping with that approach to the decorative arts that the Rookwood Pottery Company was founded in 1880 in Cincinnati by Maria Longworth Nichols Storer. She introduced a painterly tradition that influenced ceramic decoration strongly for nearly fifty years. A vase with an underglaze portrait of Chief Joseph of the Nez Percés in natural colors is an outstanding example of the output of Rookwood, which very soon became the most influential ceramics firm in the country. As might be expected, it had many imitators.

The Grueby Faience Company of Boston, founded in 1897, was another commercial enterprise that successfully employed leading designers and used advanced techniques. A pottery vase with a matte finish, made about 1900, reflects the fashion for Egyptian motifs (FIG. 36). Grueby won prizes at exhibitions both at home and abroad with such products.

A different mood prevails in a very delicate porcelain bowl made early in the twentieth century at the prestigious Syracuse atelier of Adelaide Alsop Robineau. Its rim and foot are pierced and decorated with colored incised designs; other motifs ornament the center and the outside of the bowl. Rapid industrialization and changing public taste caused most of these distinctive art potteries to cease operation one after another about the time of World War I. However, they had paved the way for the individual studio potteries of the years ahead.

THE JOAN WHITNEY PAYSON GALLERIES
PAINTINGS AND SCULPTURE

The permanent display selected from the Museum's collection of American paintings and sculpture is arranged more or less chronologically in the Joan Whitney Payson Galleries situated on the second floor of the Wing and on the mezzanine. Since its opening in 1870 the Museum has been a consistent patron of American art, and the collection of paintings now includes about 1,600 examples. The great proportion of those shown here are works from the eighteenth, nineteenth, and early twentieth centuries. The collection of sculpture is also large and varied, ranging from marble groups of heroic scale to miniature cabinet bronzes.

These holdings are constantly being enlarged and improved by new acquisitions. Virtually every artist whose work is important to the history and understanding of American art is represented by at least one example—in many instances by an outstanding one.

Even with the newly expanded facilities it is possible to exhibit only a part of this very sizable collection in the galleries and adjoining period rooms. However, the more than 300 paintings and 75 sculptures now on display clearly suggest the wealth of material from which they have been drawn. The selection provides a concise but balanced history of this country's fine arts. What remains off view will be accessible in nearby storage areas that are scheduled to open in 1981.

For all practical purposes the story of painting along the eastern seaboard of America starts with the seventeenth century. Some artist-explorers were on the scene earlier, but they did not contribute directly to the mainstream of American painting. A number of artists of limited talent but commendable zeal worked in several colonies in the 1600s. What they produced is hardly distinguishable from paintings the colonists brought with them from overseas—provincial approximations of fashionable European portraits. Conditions of life in colonial

America did not encourage specialization in any form of work and little, if any, distinction was drawn between the crafts and the fine arts. The professed artist, with or without formal training, might well turn his hand to producing shop signs or scenic and other decorations for home, ship, or store/business as need and occasion arose. Local craftsmen with no schooling or serious practice in art might on demand turn their homespun skills to limning the features of their neighbors. The eighteenth century was well along before any painter managed to live solely on his earnings as an artist.

Gallery 217

More than a dozen men, foreign-born and native, whose work typifies the best efforts of the colonial artist are represented in our collections. The English baroque style popularized by Sir Godfrey Kneller dominated American painting in the 1730s and early 1740s. Poses were derived from mezzotints; compositions had a strong sense of movement; faces were painted with directness and darkly modeled. John Smibert's portraits of *Francis Brinley* and of *Mrs. Francis Brinley and Her Son Francis* (FIG. 37) exemplify this style. Brinley was a wealthy and prominent New Englander who came to the Colonies from England in 1710. Smibert painted these likenesses in May 1729, shortly after his arrival in America. Although the artist followed the modes and standards of European art as his patrons expected him to do, basing his compositions on engravings after fashionable portraits by prominent English artists, the landscape background of Brinley's portrait is Smibert's own. It is perhaps one of the earliest painted views of Boston—a view which could be seen from the Brinley home. Born in Scotland, Smibert was apprenticed to a coach painter, studied painting in London, traveled in Italy where he copied the old masters and then returned to London where he became a successful, though minor, painter. He came to America because he thought the future of the arts was in this country, and settled in Boston because that growing little city was "the most promising field in the Colonies."

Subsequently, other emigrant English artists such as Joseph Blackburn and John Wollaston spread the elegance and artifice of the rococo style which first appeared in the Colonies in the late 1740s and early 1750s. During his relatively brief residence

FIG. 37.
*Mrs. Francis Brinley and Her Son
Francis*, by John Smibert
(1688-1751), oil on canvas, 50 by
39¼ inches, 1729.
Rogers Fund, 62.79.2

in America, from 1754 to 1763, Joseph Blackburn won the favor
of the gentry in and about Boston with such portraits as those of
Samuel Cutts and his wife. They feature the informal, bucolic
mood and pastel palette of the rococo. Blackburn was widely
admired not only for his ability to capture an accurate likeness
but also for his remarkable rendering of satin and lace.

John Singleton Copley had been painting for only two years
when Blackburn arrived in Boston, and the English-trained
artist's pictures undoubtedly inspired Copley to transform his
style. Although he was essentially self-taught, Copley had a
surpassing natural talent that enabled him to paint better pictures than any he had ever seen, including those by Blackburn.

His portrait of *Mrs. John Winthrop* (PL. 7), painted in 1773 when he was thirty-four years old, is one of ten Copleys owned by the Museum and represents his American work at its best. Here are the luminous translations of textures and surfaces into paint— the intricate fabric of lace, the sheen of silk, and the polished mahogany of the reflecting table top. These, with the strong characterization of subject and the effect of immediate presence, won Copley such prestige that he complained he hardly had time to eat his victuals as he journeyed from Boston to New York and Philadelphia fulfilling commissions. Of such brilliantly realistic likenesses John Adams once said, "You can scarcely help discussing with them, asking questions and receiving answers."

In 1782, seven years after he went to England via Italy, Copley painted the portrait of twelve-year-old Augustus Brine, midshipman in Britain's Royal Navy. In this winsome likeness, freer brushwork and dramatic lighting and ambiance reveal the early results of Copley's introduction to the old masters and the brilliant techniques of some of his English and Continental contemporaries. Copley never returned to America.

Gallery 218

Benjamin West, a self-taught Pennsylvanian exactly Copley's age, had earlier quit his native land to find greater opportunities abroad. London provided them in abundance. In 1772 West became historical painter to the king; in 1792 he succeeded the eminent Sir Joshua Reynolds as president of the Royal Academy. In his day, West was considered one of the most advanced proponents of the neoclassical mode, and he pointed the way to the Romantic style of later years. He was possibly the most widely known American artist in history, at least until James McNeill Whistler won international renown at the end of the nineteenth century. West's large allegorical canvases, such as our *Omnia Vincit Amor* or *The Power of Love in the Three Elements*, inspired such nineteenth-century American artists as Washington Allston, Rembrandt Peale, and William Sidney Mount. In his role as a teacher, West had a strong guiding influence on three generations of American painters who came to London to study with him.

One of West's American pupils, Matthew Pratt, was a fellow Pennsylvanian who as a youth had been apprenticed to a sign

painter. In 1765 he painted *The American School* (FIG. 38), a conversation piece that remains one of the major documents of colonial painting. It represents a group of young American artists working in West's London studio under the direct supervision of the master who stands, palette in hand, criticizing work by a young man who is probably Pratt.

Another of West's students, Charles Willson Peale, returned to his native land in plenty of time to join the Revolutionary forces in the field of battle, taking his painting kit along with his military gear. Peale relied on miniatures he made around this time in painting his large portraits of Revolutionary War officers. These formed the nucleus of a gallery he established in 1782 near his home in Philadelphia, and he was known as the first painter of the Revolution. In 1779 Peale accepted a com-

FIG. 38.
The American School, by Matthew Pratt (1734-1805), oil on canvas, 36 by 50¼ inches, 1765.
Gift of Samuel P. Avery, 97.29.3.

mission from the Supreme Executive Council of Pennsylvania to paint a full-length portrait of his commander in chief, General *George Washington* (FIG. 39). The result was a great success and a tribute to Peale's close observation. His many portraits of Washington are regarded as the best likenesses of him as a general. Some of the numerous replicas of the work were made for royal

FIG. 39.
George Washington, by Charles Willson Peale (1741-1827), oil on canvas, 95 by 61¾ inches, c. 1780.
Gift of Collis P. Huntington, 97.33.

PLATE 7. (OPPOSITE)
Mrs. John Winthrop, by John Singleton Copley (1738-1815), oil on canvas, 35½ by 28¾ inches, 1773.
Morris K. Jesup Fund, 31.109.

PLATE **8.**

The Sortie Made by the Garrison of Gibraltar, by John Trumbull (1756-1843), oil on canvas, 70½ by 106 inches, 1789.

Purchase, Pauline V. Fullerton Bequest, Mr. and Mrs. James Walter Carter Gift, Mr. and Mrs. Raymond J. Horowitz Gift, Erving Wolf Foundation Gift, Vain and Harry Fish Foundation, Inc. Gift, Gift of Hanson K. Corning, by exchange, and Maria DeWitt Jesup and Morris K. Jesup Funds, 1976.332.

PLATE **9.** (RIGHT)

General Louis-Marie, Vicomte de Noailles, by Gilbert Stuart (1755-1828), oil on canvas, 51 by 39 inches, 1798.

Purchase, Henry R. Luce Gift, Elihu Root, Jr. Bequest, Rogers Fund, Maria DeWitt Jesup Fund, Morris K. Jesup Fund, and Charles and Anita Blatt Gift, 1970.262.

66

palaces abroad. The Museum owns one of these much coveted copies, perhaps made on order from Martha Washington. The general stands in front of a cold and desolate river landscape which represents Trenton, New Jersey, an area Peale had visited on a recent sketching trip. The colonial American flag flutters in the background.

In his long life Peale was not only a prolific and versatile artist, but also an author, a naturalist, an inventor, a saddler, a silversmith, an engraver, and a museum director. He married three times and sired seventeen children, some of whom became artists in their own right. As a man, Charles Willson Peale was one of the most unusual and engaging of all American artists and a representative of the rationalism of eighteenth-century enlightenment.

John Trumbull, the wellborn son of a governor of Connecticut and a young Harvard graduate, also served in the Revolution, as an aide-de-camp to Washington. However, in the first year of the war he quit the army in a pique over what he hypersensitively considered a point of honor. Subsequently he went to London to study with Benjamin West. Trumbull's large historical paintings, such as those memorializing the events of the Revolution, that decorate the rotunda of the Capitol at Washington, are the most conspicuous examples of his art. These are based on earlier studies including sensitive portraits, done from life whenever possible, of the principal actors in his scenes.

Possibly Trumbull's most successful work of this heroic order, *The Sortie Made by the Garrison of Gibraltar* (PL. 8), painted in 1789 when he was in London, depicts an episode during the three-year siege of the English fortress by French and Spanish forces. In 1781, under the command of General Elliott, the British had destroyed an entire line of the enemy's counterworks in a nighttime foray. Trumbull chose to dramatize the moment when the gallant Spaniard Don José Barboza, although mortally wounded, refused British help because that would have meant complete surrender to the enemy.

Most of West's numerous American pupils returned to their homeland with developed skills that established fresh standards in post-Revolutionary American art. One of the most celebrated of these repatriates was the witty, urbane, and bibulous Gilbert Stuart, who mastered a highly distinctive painterly

FIG. 40.
George Washington, by Gilbert
Stuart (1755-1828), oil on canvas, 30¼ by 25¼ inches, 1795 or
shortly after.

Rogers Fund, 07.160.

style of portraiture. His vivid and idealized likenesses earned
him considerable prestige in England and attracted wide patronage in the new Republic. Omitting accessory paraphernalia
of the kind that inform and enlighten Copley's paintings, Stuart
reduced detail to a minimum, often skimping even bodies and
backgrounds.

Of his innumerable portraits of Washington, the Museum
owns a fine early example (FIG. 40), apparently done in part
from life, that represents Stuart's classical American style in its
pure form. This canvas is known as the Gibbs-Channing-Avery
Washington, with reference to its former owners. It has been
said often that so well known have such likenesses of the first
president become that if he should return to earth he would
have to resemble Stuart's portraits to be recognized. Another of
the more than twenty paintings by this artist in our collection, a
likeness of *James Monroe*, fifth president of the United States, is

the only known survivor of a set of half-length portraits of the first five American presidents that Stuart produced for John Doggett, a Boston art dealer, about 1818 to 1820. It is both more elaborate and more spirited than most of his late work.

Stuart also painted a memorable group of full-length portraits of Washington and some of his eminent contemporaries. One of the latter is a likeness of *Louis-Marie, Vicomte de Noailles* (PL. 9), painted at Philadelphia in 1798. The Vicomte was a dashing young French aristocrat and brother-in-law of Lafayette, who, among other adventures on two continents, had served with the French troops in the American Revolution. He is shown here in the colorful uniform of the brigadier general commanding the first regiment of Chasseurs à Cheval d'Alsace. He stands beside his horse on a bluff beneath which his cavalry troops march in parade.

Gallery 219

For almost a century, one or another of the extraordinary Peale family was painting pictures. About 1822, Charles Willson Peale's brother James, who also had served in the Revolutionary army, produced *Balsam Apple and Vegetables* (FIG. 41). This is a remarkably convincing still life in which the varied shapes,

FIG. 41.
Still life: Balsam Apple and Vegetables, by James Peale (1749-1831), oil on canvas, 20¼ by 26½ inches, probably 1820s.
Maria DeWitt Jesup Fund, 39.52.

FIG. 42. (OPPOSITE)
The Muse—Susan Walker Morse,
by Samuel F. B. Morse (1791-
1872), oil on canvas, 73¾ by
57⅝ inches, 1835-1837.
Bequest of Herbert L. Pratt, 45.62.1.

textures, colors, and all but the very taste of cabbage, eggplant, okra, tomatoes, and the balsam apple are presented in an opulent composition. James's nephew and Charles Willson's son Raphaelle Peale also created still lifes. His *Still Life with Cake* is one of this group that, in their precise drawing and highly illusionistic coloring, remind us of Dutch and Flemish paintings of a century or two earlier, and that are as fine as any ever produced in this country.

In the years following the conclusion of the War of 1812, the scene shifts to a generation of artists who, like Raphaelle Peale, were too young to remember the Revolution and who, for the most part, had the advantage of solid professional training. It was this generation of painters who sowed the seeds of romanticism that found fertile ground in America and that developed into a wide and varied flowering of talent as the nation spread out across the continent. The spirit in which these men approached their subjects is brilliantly demonstrated in the canvases of Sanuel F. B. Morse, Thomas Sully, Charles C. Ingham, George P. A. Healy, and a score of others whose work is represented in the Museum's collection.

The Muse (FIG. 42), Morse's sensitive likeness of his eldest daughter, Susan, in a pensive mood, was one of the last and most skillful of his portraits before this artist put aside his brushes forever to devote himself to developing the electric telegraph. That decision resulted in a great loss to American art and a great benefit to American science. Sully's appealing likeness of the young *Queen Victoria*, a study for a commissioned work that he painted from life in 1838, demonstrates the artist's remarkable facility in handling pigment.

In his painting of *Amelia Palmer*, a wealthy young Connecticut heiress, the Irish-born Ingham combined portraiture, still life, and landscape with the highly polished, miniaturelike technique that won him fashionable patronage in the decades before the Civil War. Healy's portrait of *Euphemia White Van Rensselaer*, daughter of "the last patroon," was painted in 1842 in Paris, where the artist had been studying for the past eight years. Although the Boston-born Healy was then still in his twenties, this is one of the finest works of his long cosmopolitan career. During the course of that career he painted several portraits of Abraham Lincoln and one of the "citizen king" of France, Louis Philippe, who commissioned him to paint likenesses of outstanding American statesmen for the royal collection.

In the meantime, other artists in America were taking a close look at the common man in his rural and village habitat and on the western rivers and plains, reporting his activities in a spirit of flattering candor. In William Sidney Mount's quiet and genial pictures of his Long Island neighbors, as in his *Cider Making* (FIG. 43), there is an intimacy, and at times humor, that reflects a bond between the artist and a broad public. Farther west, George Caleb Bingham recorded the rough habits of the now almost legendary rivermen on their barges and flatboats, the hurly-burly of election activities, and, as in our *Fur Traders Descending the Missouri* (PL. 10), occasional poetic glimpses of a passing moment in the life of the frontier. These men won large and appreciative audiences with their commonplace subjects so

FIG. 43.
Cider Making, by William Sidney Mount (1807-1868), oil on canvas, 27 by 34⅛ inches, 1841.

Purchase, Charles Allen Munn Bequest, 1966 (66.126).

simply and realistically construed. With the rising tide of democracy, American painting became a popular art.

By the middle years of the nineteenth century an increasing number of American sculptors were practicing their art as full-time professionals. Many of them learned and worked in Rome and Florence, where sculptors from other parts of the world also gathered to study statues of the classical past and the Renaissance. For the most part the output of the Americans consisted of portrait busts—solidly realistic likenesses in a neoclassical manner.

A characteristic and outstanding instance of this approach is the bust of *Andrew Jackson* by Hiram Powers (FIG. 44), a Vermonter who in 1835 modeled the grizzled, toothless war veteran

FIG. 44.
Andrew Jackson, by Hiram Powers (1805-1873), marble, height 34½ inches, 1837.

Gift of Mrs. Frances V. Nash, 94.14.

and president to the life, but draped his shoulders with a Roman toga. The marble version was cut in Italy whither Powers went in 1837, never to return to America.

In 1844 Edward Augustus Brackett, a New Englander who did not go to Italy, portrayed the eminent painter *Washington Allston*, again combining classic reserve and forthright realism. His study was based on a death mask of the subject taken a year earlier. The antithesis of this quiet neoclassicism is the more energetic *Genius of Mirth* by Thomas Crawford. It represents a gleeful little boy dancing and clapping a pair of cymbals. Crawford worked principally in Italy and he, too, was celebrated in his time.

Gallery 220

In the middle decades of the last century American artists were opening vistas that had been barely perceived by Stuart, Trumbull, and other early portraitists. These years saw the beginnings of a significant tradition in landscape painting, notably in the canvases of an unorganized fraternity of able painters known as the Hudson River school. In their meticulously detailed yet lyrical pictures of the hills and lakes, the valleys and rivers of their still semiwild continent, these men faithfully portrayed the beauty and grandeur of the American land, as Washington Irving, James Fenimore Cooper, and William Cullen Bryant were celebrating it in their writings.

Thomas Cole, a virtually self-taught English immigrant, early developed into a superb landscapist whose work had a strong influence on this group of painters. His panoramic vistas, such as *View from Mount Holyoke, Massachusetts, after a Thunderstorm—The Oxbow* (PL. 11), are expert and immensely appealing renderings of natural scenes, and they won immediate popular applause. Asher B. Durand, an engraver turned painter and another founding member of the Hudson River school, often explored the Catskills with Cole, sketchbook in hand. *The Beeches* (FIG. 45) is characteristic of the landscapes that he produced in the 1840s and that found a ready market among collectors of the day. His *In the Woods*, painted in 1855, was called the finest of his works by some critics of the time. Throughout his long life, Durand's early training as an engraver gave his works a precision and clarity admirably suited to a faithful representation of nature. Thomas Doughty was considered by some to be a founder of the Hudson River school

PLATE 11.
View from Mount Holyoke, Massachusetts, after a Thunderstorm – The
Oxbow, by Thomas Cole (1801-1848), oil on canvas, 51½ by 76 inches,
1836.

Gift of Mrs. Russell Sage, 08.228.

PLATE 12.
Heart of the Andes, by Frederic Edwin Church (1826-1900), oil on canvas, 66⅛ by 119¼ inches, 1859.
Bequest of Margaret E. Dows, 1909 (09.95).

along with Cole, although he did not frequent the Hudson River area until his later years. His *On the Hudson*, with its tiny figure in the foreground, is a poetic expression of the joys of solitude in surroundings of natural beauty, a recurrent theme in Doughty's work.

A selection of sculptures roughly contemporary with the paintings is included in these galleries of landscapes. While painters were looking for new directions in the American world about them, many sculptors continued to cling to the classical ideal, which deterred fresh advances in their art. Henry Kirke Brown, a portrait painter turned sculptor, fashioned a likeness of *Thomas Cole* in the neoclassical style, complete with toga.

FIG. 45.
The Beeches, by Asher B. Durand (1796-1886), oil on canvas, 60⅜ by 48⅛ inches, 1845.
Bequest of Maria DeWitt Jesup, 15.30.59.

FIG. 46.
Autumn Oaks, by George Inness
(1825-1894), oil on canvas, 21⅛
by 30¼ inches, c. 1875.
Gift of George I. Seney, 87.8.8.

Gallery 221

A considerable number of canvases by such very capable artists as Frederic Edwin Church, John F. Kensett, Sanford R. Gifford, Martin Johnson Heade, Fitz Hugh Lane, and George Inness, illustrate the further development of landscape painting in the years surrounding the Civil War. In benign and remarkably atmospheric works such as *Autumn Oaks* (FIG. 46), the

FIG. 47.
The Coming Storm, by Martin Johnson Heade (1819-1904), oil on canvas, 26 by 39 inches, 1878.
Gift of Erving Wolf Foundation, and Mr. and Mrs. Erving Wolf, 1975.160.

largely self-taught Inness recorded the smiling aspects of the
American countryside after the disasters of the war had passed
from the scene. A preoccupation with the effects of light and
atmosphere earned a sizable group of these men the name of
luminists. Kensett's *Lake George*, painted in 1869, is a subtle
counterpoint of land, water, and shimmering atmosphere. In

The Coming Storm (FIG. 47), Heade reveals a similar intense love
of nature and light. Isolated figures and a single white sail under
the threatening dark cloud produce an almost surrealistic impression, which is typical of this artist's work.

In the 1850s Fitz Hugh Lane, America's first native-born
marine painter of real merit, was producing some of his finest
canvases. His *Stage Fort Across Gloucester Harbor* (FIG. 48) is one
of the serene and spacious New England waterfront views he
knew so intimately and recorded in subtle colors and with
highly skilled draughtsmanship. Lane was sensitive to the
changing moods of sea and sky and he thoroughly understood

FIG. 48.

*Stage Fort Across Gloucester Har-
bor*, by Fitz Hugh Lane (1804-
1865), oil on canvas, 38 by 60
inches, 1862.

Purchase, Rogers and Fletcher Funds,
Erving and Joyce Wolf Fund, Raymond
J. Horowitz Gift, Bequest of Richard
De Wolfe Brixey, by exchange, and
John Osgood and Elizabeth Amis
Cameron Blanchard Memorial Fund,
1978 (1978.203).

FIG. 49.
*The Rocky Mountains, Lander's
Peak*, by Albert Bierstadt
(1830-1902), oil on canvas,
73¼ by 120¾ inches, 1863.
Rogers Fund, 07.123.

marine architecture. His work had a strong influence on younger painters of his day.

Albert Bierstadt strove for spectacular effects in dynamic depictions of the rugged western mountains, which he made familiar to most Americans for the first time. Such grandiose panoramas as *The Rocky Mountains*, freely worked up in his New York studio from studies made in the field, brought Bierstadt higher prices than any American artist had yet received for his work. When it was first shown in New York, this more or less synthetic creation received a tumultuous public welcome.

With such huge, impressive visions of the western scene it might be said that the discovery of America by its artists was almost complete. To satisfy his wish to record more remote and exotic natural spectacles, Thomas Cole's pupil Frederic Edwin Church journeyed to South America. There he sketched volcanic mountains and such panoramic views as the Museum's *The Heart of the Andes* (PL. 12). This painting is hung opposite Bierstadt's *The Rocky Mountains* (FIG. 49), as they were originally

shown at the New York Sanitary Fair of 1864. Church also traveled to the frozen wastes of the Arctic with its mountains of ice, and to distant Greece. He worked his sketches into finished canvases upon returning to his studio.

A new generation of sculptors came on the scene in the post-Civil War decade. Their work, though still in the neoclassical mode, shows the increased regard for realism that was affecting all the arts. William Henry Rinehart, perhaps the best of this generation, spent much of his professional life abroad. When he died in 1874 he was still at work on the marble group of *Latona*, goddess of the night, with Apollo and Diana, her children by Jupiter; it was completed after his death.

The realism of Rinehart's work was carried a long step forward by John Quincy Adams Ward in his bronze *Indian Hunter* (FIG. 50), in which he depicted a stalking brave with his hunting dog, and which he had cast in 1860 following a trip west to study native Indians on their own heath. A few years later an enlarged version of this model was placed in Central Park, where it may still be seen. Much the same naturalism characterizes the bronze portrait of *Sanford R. Gifford* by the Irish-born artist Launt Thompson.

Gallery 222

Ward's bronze full-length statuette of the noted American clergyman and orator *Henry Ward Beecher*, shown in this gallery, served as a study for the Beecher monument in Borough Hall Square, Brooklyn, where it was erected in 1891.

During these postwar decades two entirely different, strongly independent painters, each utterly candid in his vision of the world about him, were producing pictures whose interest has continued to grow with time. The canvases of Winslow Homer and Thomas Eakins are today rated among the finest the New World has produced. Homer's work is richly represented in the collection and spans his entire artistic career. His early paintings of Civil War scenes, such as *Prisoners from the Front* (FIG. 51), and of New England rural life, such as *Snap the Whip*, are realistic reporting that seemed to some critics of the time rough and homely, to others straightforward and powerful. The former, painted in 1866, shows a group of bedraggled but proud Confederate prisoners facing their Union captor. It is a

FIG. 50.
Indian Hunter, by John Quincy Adams Ward (1830-1910), bronze, height 16 inches, 1860.
Morris K. Jesup Fund, 1973.257.

FIG. 51.
Prisoners from the Front, by
Winslow Homer (1836-1910),
oil on canvas, 24 by 38 inches,
1866.

Gift of Mrs. Frank B. Porter, 22.207.

very sensitive reflection on an episode that Homer is thought to have observed as a war correspondent at the front during the tragic conflict. The second of these subjects pictures in equally realistic fashion the playful outdoor antics of freckle-faced Yankee children during a recess from their one-room schoolhouse.

In his later works, such as *The Gulf Stream* and *Northeaster* (Frontispiece), Homer tended toward greater austerity and more impressionistic rendering. For him the practice of art was the answer to a compulsive instinct that, like mending the fence and gathering the hay, had its right moment. He had no teachers of consequence and no pupils—he was one of the great independent artists of his day to win recognition in his own lifetime.

Two other sculptures shown in this gallery are by Augustus Saint-Gaudens, who was one of the leading figures of the American art world in the final decades of the nineteenth century. One is a portrait of *Admiral David Glasgow Farragut*, a study for the Farragut Monument in Madison Square which, when it was unveiled in 1881, immediately established the reputation of the sculptor. The other is an idealized but forbidding bronze figure of *The Puritan* (FIG. 56), Bible in hand, whose stance and mien suggest the unquestionable righteousness of our venerable ancestors.

Gallery 223

In this large L-shaped adjacent gallery will be displayed a rotating selection of material from our collection that parallels and supplements the permanent exhibits in the surrounding painting galleries. The one fixed and the principal feature of this room is the enormous canvas *Washington Crossing the Delaware* by the German-born Emanuel Leutze (FIG. 52). Generations of Americans have formed visual impressions of our country's early past from sentimentalized reconstructions of colonial history produced by painters, sculptors, and novelists of the nineteenth century. Leutze's work, painted in 1851, is a conspicuous example of such romantic imagery. Although it is inaccurate in many historical details, it has become a widely accepted symbol of Washington's heroic coup on Christmas night in 1776. It is Leutze's most famous picture, so laden with patriotic sentiment that it is almost beside the point to attempt

FIG. 52.
Washington Crossing the Delaware, by Emanuel Leutze (1816-1868), oil on canvas, 12 feet, 5 inches by 21 feet, 3 inches, 1851.

Gift of John Stewart Kennedy, 97.34.

any esthetic criticism—except to recall that it is highly representative of a school of romantic painting that flourished during
the middle years of the last century at Düsseldorf, Germany,
where Leutze was living when he composed it. Worthington
Whittredge, one of the American artists present while Leutze
was working in Germany, posed for the figures of both Washington and the steersman.

Gallery 224

In the decades that followed the Civil War a large number
of painters and sculptors, some European trained, others
homebred, contributed in different ways to the changing patterns of American art. When he was working in the Hague,
Eastman Johnson was hailed as the "American Rembrandt,"
and he was offered the post of court painter. However, he chose
to return to his native land, where his particular talents quickly
won him wide recognition and steady patronage. No detail is
neglected in *The Hatch Family* (FIG. 53), dated 1871—a realistic

PLATE 14.
Arques-La-Bataille, by John H. Twachtman (1853-1902), oil on canvas,
60 by 78⅞ inches, 1885.

Morris K. Jesup Fund, 68.52.

group portrait of fifteen members of this prominent New York
family in the opulently furnished library of their Park Avenue
residence. The baby, born after the rest of the picture was
finished, was dubbed in last by the artist to bring the record up
to date. Johnson considered this his masterpiece.

The paintings of the Philadelphian Thomas Eakins (FIG. 54),
Homer's close contemporary and an equally distinguished
painter, are shown in the balcony gallery. Eakins displayed
stubborn persistence in painting people—largely his fellow
Philadelphians— and things as he saw them, with candor which
was more uncompromising than most critics of his day could
accept. When he died in 1916 his work was relatively unknown.

The Metropolitan Museum acquired some of its paintings by
Eakins from the artist and his wife, Susan Hannah Macdowell
Eakins, who was also a painter, and these constitute the nucleus
of our impressive collection. Eakins's *Max Schmitt in a Single
Scull (The Champion Single Sculls)*, his reflective full-length portrait of Louis Kenton, entitled *The Thinker* (FIG. 55), and his
Portrait of a Lady [Mrs. Eakins] *with a Setter Dog* (PL. 13) brilliantly demonstrate the absolute integrity and high degree of
technical competence with which he rendered his chosen subjects. These qualities sent his reputation soaring after he was
quietly in his grave.

There is also featured in this gallery a small but distinguished
group of bronzes and paintings that represent life in the American West during the final decades of the nineteenth century,
when that region was completing an epic cycle. The frontier, so
long a significant feature of American experience, was de-
clared closed in 1890. With some good reason Frederic Remington considered himself *the* artist-reporter of the rapidly van-
ishing ways of life along these vast borderlands where army
troopers, cowboys, and Indians acted out the finale of an almost
legendary drama. Remington's action-charged pictures, which
remain a vivid guide for those who try to visualize the passing of
the wild West, are typified by *Cavalry Charge on the Southern
Plains*. Theodore Roosevelt predicted that the cowboy would
live for all time in the bronze figures of Remington, such as
Comin' Through the Rye (FIG. 57), which could be translated
"coming to town for a spree," and *The Bronco Buster*. After the
Indian had been completely subdued and pushed aside, nostal-

FIG. 54.
Thomas Eakins, by Samuel Mur-
ray (1870-1941), bronze, height
9 inches, 1907.
Rogers Fund, 23.155.

Gallery 224

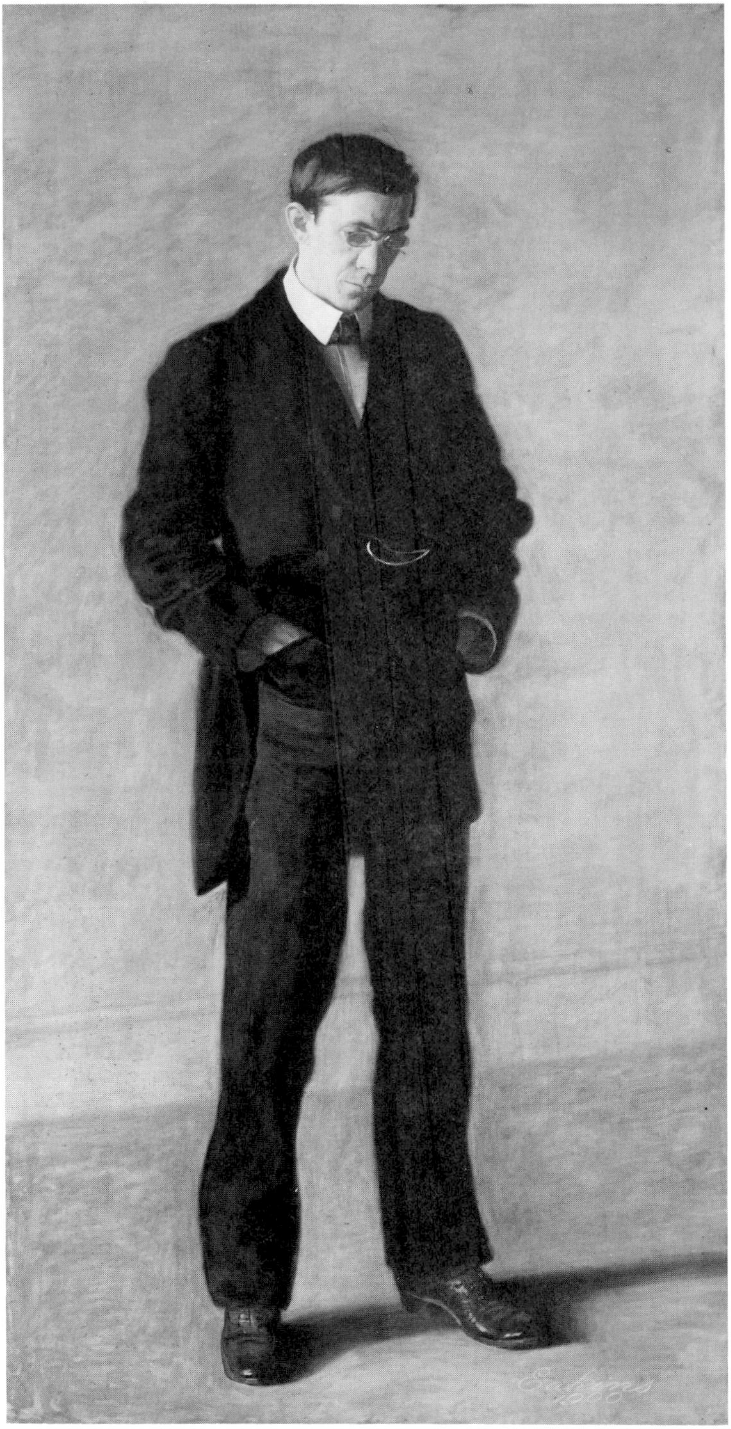

FIG. 55.
The Thinker: Portrait of Louis Kenton, by Thomas Eakins (1844-1916), oil on canvas, 82 by 42 inches, 1900.
John Stewart Kennedy Fund, 17.172.

gia led to his re-creation in a new image, a noble red man tragically and heroically facing the coming invasion of whites, as represented in Hermon MacNeil's bronze *A Chief of the Multnomah Tribe.*

A complete antithesis of these realistic western subjects is found in the brooding, visionary canvases of Ralph Albert Blakelock and Albert Pinkham Ryder shown in the adjacent space. Blakelock's *Indian Encampment* presents the darkling image of a forest, a vision of a mysterious but beautiful world that haunted the artist's unstable mind and to which he returned time and again. The difficulties of selling his work contributed to Blakelock's tragic madness, and he spent virtually his last twenty years in a sanatorium. Ironically, toward the end of his life his paintings fetched ever-higher prices in the market place, with no benefit to the impoverished artist or his family.

FIG. 56.
The Puritan, by Augustus Saint-Gaudens (1848-1907), bronze, height 31 inches, 1887; this cast 1899.
Bequest of Jacob Ruppert, 39.65.53.

FIG. 57.
Comin' Through the Rye, by Frederic Remington (1861-1909), bronze, height 27⅜ inches, c. 1902.
Bequest of Jacob Ruppert, 39.65.44.

FIG. **58.**
Moonlight Marine, by Albert
Ryder (1847-1917), oil on wood,
11⅜ by 12 inches, n.d.
Samuel D. Lee Fund, 34.55.

As Blakelock's vision was haunted by the forest, Ryder's was haunted by the sea—the sea in its awesome and somber loneliness, as it had never before been painted. The lyrical intensity of Ryder's vision gives an emotional force to *Moonlight Marine* (FIG. 58), a stark view of a vast clouded sky, a vast tossing sea, and a small phantom vessel. Ryder was inspired by nature but paid little heed to detail. His seascapes were creations of a subjective, deeply personal inner vision. He sometimes worked for years on his pictures, often on several simultaneously. He even reworked some he had already sold, in an endless struggle to create a unique pictorial statement.

In the adjacent space, there is a display of trompe-l'œil painting. These still-life pictures, so popular in America during the 1880s and 1890s, were compositions painted to deceive the eye by cleverly creating an illusion of three-dimensional reality on a flat painted surface. During the last quarter of the nineteenth century several virtuoso American artists, led and inspired by William Michael Harnett, depicted disparate objects seemingly arranged at random in a shallow space. They carried this sort of visual trickery to a point that almost deceives the eye with simulated textures, faithfully rendered colors, and careful drawing. Hence the French term *trompe l'œil* ("fool the eye") is commonly applied to such ingenious exercises. The miscellaneous paraphernalia so artfully represented in Harnett's *The Artist's Card Rack* (FIG. 59), in Haberle's *A Bachelor's Drawer,* and in Peto's *Old Souvenirs* truly seem to be real and tangible rather than flat imitations.

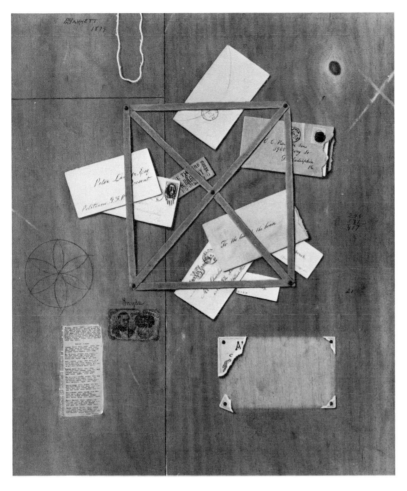

FIG. 59.
The Artist's Card Rack, by
William Michael Harnett
(1848-1892), oil on canvas, 30 by
25 inches, 1879.
Morris K. Jesup Fund, 66.13.

Gallery M1

In 1855, James Abbott McNeill Whistler of Massachusetts
had left his job with the Coastal and Geodetic survey and gone
to Paris to study art. In 1859 he proceeded to London, where he
became a great celebrity. This elegant wit and accomplished
painter insisted that art was for its own sake, that painting was
based on the intrinsic interest of formal, decorative, and significant designs in color. To disassociate them from their osten-
sible subjects, he termed his paintings "arrangements," "noc-
turnes," and "symphonies." Thus he referred to his portrait of
Theodore Duret as *Arrangement in Flesh Colour and Black* (FIG. 60)
and to his most popular portrait, that of his own aging mother,

commonly known as "Whistler's Mother," as *Arrangement in Grey and Black, No. 1.* Whistler had no pupils, but the influence of his esthetic theories was considerable.

Down the staircase and on the mezzanine are arranged impressionist through twentieth-century works. The painters of many of these, like Whistler, preferred to live out their professional careers abroad. John Singer Sargent, a younger contemporary of Whistler's and a complete cosmopolitan, chose to settle in London after studying and working for a period of years in Paris. His success as a fashionable portraitist was extraordinary; to be "done" by Sargent was considered a distinction and a privilege, and well worth the very high fee. His portrait of Mme. Pierre Gautreau entitled *Madame X* (FIG.61), is a striking characterization of a celebrated beauty and a masterpiece of economical expression. Sargent himself offered the canvas to the Museum in 1916, writing "I suppose it is the best thing I have done." Since then the Museum has acquired more than a dozen other examples of this artist's work in oil, such as *The Wyndham Sisters* and *Mr. and Mrs. Isaac Newton Phelps Stokes.* The latter painting shows a psychological penetration which appears in Sargent's works only rarely. Later in life he found welcome relief from fashionable portraiture in landscapes and other watercolors of dazzling charm, which are well represented in our collection. It is no heresy to prefer these private exercises of Sargent to his commissioned portraits. Painting for himself for a change, unhampered by any need to satisfy a client, employing a medium natural to his quick and fluid style of recording impressions, his response was so personal and immediate that it is impossible to remain indifferent to these works.

The work of Cecilia Beaux, a Philadelphia artist, has often been compared with that of Sargent. The broad and fluid brushwork seen in our *Ernesta with Nurse* suggests the reason for this. Beaux also studied in Paris, but returned to settle in New York and became recognized as one of the most accomplished portrait painters of her day.

In the years following the Civil War other American artists swarmed to Europe to savor a rich variety of experience in countries of the Old World, there to find fresh inspiration and instruction in their art. They returned to America from Munich, Paris, and other art centers with new techniques and more cosmopolitan outlooks. They were confident that, upon

FIG. 60.

*Arrangement in Flesh Colour and
Black: Portrait of Theodore Duret*,
by James Abbott McNeill
Whistler (1834-1903), oil on
canvas, 76⅛ by 35¾
inches, c. 1883.

Wolfe Fund, Catharine Lorillard Wolfe
Collection, 13.20.

FIG. 61.
Madame X, by John Singer Sargent (1856-1925), oil on canvas, 82⅛ by 43¼ inches, 1884.
Arthur Hoppock Hearn Fund, 16.53.

their return, they would form the advance guard in creating important new developments in American painting. A sizable number of them had been markedly influenced by the work of the French Impressionists and actually referred to themselves as "impressionists."

Mary Cassatt was a Philadelphia heiress with impeccable social credentials. She was the only American artist who became an established member of the Impressionist group in Paris. She worked with Degas and learned from him, Manet, and other French painters, but she imitated none of them. She was not interested in important personages for her subject matter and treated many of her sitters so impersonally that few of them are even identified. This is not the case with *Lady at*

FIG. 62.
Lady at the Tea Table, by Mary Cassatt (1844-1926), oil on canvas, 29 by 24 inches, 1885.
Gift of Mary Cassatt, 23.101.

the Tea Table (Mrs. Robert Moore Riddle) (FIG. 62) or *The Cup of Tea*, in which the sitter is Lydia Cassatt, the artist's sister. Cassatt's numerous glowing depictions of women and their small children are well known. She had an important influence on the development of American taste—at least the taste of her wealthy compatriots, whom she introduced to the works of many significant European artists, past as well as present, and advised in their purchases.

A born Vermonter, Theodore Robinson spent several years in Giverny, a small Normandy village on the Seine. There he enjoyed a close friendship with his neighbor and mentor, the eminent French painter Claude Monet. In *A Bird's-Eye View* (FIG. 63), Robinson painted Giverny from a steep bluff that rises from the river valley. Although in a real sense impressionistic, the canvas nevertheless shows a firm definition of forms that was traditional in American landscape painting. Returning from France, the artist had to adjust his sights to the different realities of his native scene and atmosphere. The light in this country was different from that in France; and the progressive commotion of America seemed to offer only prosaic

FIG. 63.

A Bird's-Eye View, by Theodore Robinson (1854-1896), oil on canvas, 26 by 32½ inches, 1889.

Gift of George A. Hearn, 10.64.9.

PLATE 15.
At the Seaside, by William Merritt Chase (1849-1916), oil on canvas, 20
by 34 inches, c. 1892.

Bequest of Miss Adelaide Milton de Groot (1876-1967), 1967 (67.187.123).

PLATE 16.
Office in a Small City, by Edward Hopper (1882-1967), oil on canvas, 28 by 40 inches, 1953.

George A. Hearn Fund, 53.183.

counterparts to the clustered stone dwellings and picturesquely costumed natives of Normandy and Brittany.

During his sojourn in France, Childe Hassam learned the
technique and the palette of the Impressionists: to lay on his
canvases the brilliant synthetic pigments that were now available, in separate, small flakes for the eye of the observer to mix
in his own way. This he did in his painting *Spring Morning in the
Heart of the City*. Here as in other examples of his work he did
not emphasize color vibrations at the expense of the forms he
depicted.

The broad contingent of American impressionists and post-
impressionists also included such disparate and talented artists
as Maurice Prendergast, Edmund C. Tarbell, Julian Alden
Weir, and John Henry Twachtman. Twachtman pictured
Arques-La-Bataille (PL. 14), a site near Dieppe on the Normandy
coast, in a subtle orchestration of subdued colors. Delicate
grays, greens, and blues were thinly and broadly applied in a
manner that evokes an image of the landscape rather than
defines it, and recalls the tonal harmonies of Whistler.

Another influential artist, William Merritt Chase, instructed
many art students. While studying in Munich early in his
professional career, he worked very successfully in a broad
manner that recalled the slashing brush strokes of Frans Hals,
Peter Paul Rubens, and Diego Velázquez. Back in America,
Chase lightened his palette and in outdoor scenes such as *At the
Seaside* (PL. 15) and *Mrs. Chase in Prospect Park*, applied brilliant
colors with a masterful technique and enormous zest.

About the turn of the century a number of American women
had established reputations as sculptors; works by two of them
are shown in these galleries. Like Mary Cassatt, Bessie Potter
Vonnoh dwelt on the warm relationship between mother and
child, exploring this theme in small bronzes such as *The Young
Mother*, which won her an award at the Paris Exposition of 1900.
In 1908 Vonnoh's contemporary Edith Woodman Burroughs
created a moody likeness of the American artist, author, and
teacher *John La Farge* in the last years of his life. Our bronze was
acquired the year of La Farge's death. Gutzon Borglum's
statuette of the famed British art critic and author *John Ruskin* is
also on display in this gallery. The sculptor had met Ruskin
earlier and portrayed him as he then saw the old man, "drawn
into himself," full of confidence, but sad.

The last of the painting galleries is devoted to a small selection of early to mid-twentieth-century art. Those years witnessed remarkable changes in the arts, although this selection represents only a sampling which focuses on the continuation of

FIG. 64.
Central Park in Winter, by William Glackens (1870-1938), oil on canvas, 25 by 30 inches, 1905.
George A. Hearn Fund, 21.164.

the realist tradition–rather than the full range of innovations– in American art. At the start, new and challenging forces were making themselves felt. In 1908 eight artists showed their work at the Macbeth Gallery in New York. Their exhibition was a revolt of sorts. They based their work on the older Continental realists like Hals, Velázquez, and Manet, and challenged the current, somewhat idealized, artistic trends of the academies. The Eight, as they will probably always be called–Robert Henri, John Sloan, George Luks, Maurice Prendergast, Ernest Lawson, Everett Shinn, Arthur B. Davies, and William Glackens–were all individuals in their styles and techniques. They were determined that the artist should have freedom and opportunity to express his message in his own way. They saw in the ordinary person and the commonplace scene, even among the

ash cans of the teeming cities, a poetry worthy of the artist's
brush.

Paintings by all eight of these men are represented in our
collection. The catholicity they showed in their choice of subject matter, which drew censure at the time, is clearly revealed
in several disparate canvases. Henri's broadly painted *The Mas-
querade Dress* (portrait of his wife) reflects his admiration for the
old-master tradition. Sloan's *Dust Storm, Fifth Avenue* tran-
scribes a gusty moment's confusion on a Manhattan street.
Central Park in Winter (FIG. 64), painted by Glackens in 1905,
records a happy anecdote apprehended quickly without resort
to any unnecessary detail. In an entirely different vein Arthur
B. Davies's *Unicorns* (FIG. 65), probably his most famous work,
presents a scene withdrawn from reality into a tranquil, lyrical
world of the artist's imagination.

The Eight had an impact on several young realists. George
Bellows, for example, who chose to be a professional painter
instead of a professional baseball player, and who is perhaps
best remembered for his lithographs of prize fights, took part in
the "new" realism advocated by The Eight. His *Up The Hudson*
(FIG. 66) suggests the drama of New York's great river as it flows
southward toward the swarming metropolis the artist liked so
much. With these several examples, chosen from a large

FIG. 65.
Unicorns, by Arthur B. Davies
(1862-1928), oil on canvas, 18¼
by 40¼ inches, 1906.
Bequest of Lizzie P. Bliss, 31.67.12.

number of others, it becomes clear that what seemed a rebellion early in the century is seen today as simply another link in the long chain of American realism.

The work of Maxfield Parrish, represented here by *The Errant Pan*, painted about 1915, is strikingly different from that of any of the other artists considered in these pages. For almost two decades Parrish created idealized fantasies that were characterized by almost photographic detail, unnaturally luminous colors, and impeccably finished surfaces. These subjects were reproduced in millions of color prints and won him an enormous public audience throughout the land. In the 1920s his vogue reached epidemic proportions.

At the famous Armory Show of 1913 Arthur B. Davies and Walt Kuhn, with the assistance of other vanguard American

FIG. 66.
Up the Hudson, by George Bellows (1882-1925), oil on canvas, 35⅞ by 48⅛ inches, 1908.
Gift of Hugo Reisinger, 11.17.

artists, exhibited modern art both American and foreign. The major impact of that great exhibition came from the international section. For the first time, Americans at large experienced the shock of postimpressionism, fauvism, expressionism, cubism, and other phases of abstract painting and sculpture which had developed in Europe over the preceding twenty or thirty years. From then on "modern art" became a phrase to conjure with in this country, a battle cry that continues to evoke strong feelings ranging from great enthusiasm to utter revulsion. Virtually all the paintings in this gallery that have not yet been mentioned date from after the Armory Show.

As early as 1910 Arthur Dove, having just spent two years in Paris, said that he had given up "trying to express an idea by stating innumerable little facts." His *Hand Sewing Machine*, painted on heavy metal in oils with applied cloth, is a witty example of how he took commonplace objects as points of departure for inventions in pattern, leaving only a minimal visual hint of some nominal subject. In *Cow's Skull* Georgia O'Keeffe shows how she found forms in the surrounding world that could be restructured by inspired imagination into new and suggestive harmonies of shapes and colors. An elaborate head of O'Keeffe made in 1927 by the French-born sculptor Gaston Lachaise is exhibited in this gallery. The crisp formal patterns of industrial America are reduced to an abstract yet clearly stated representation in Charles Sheeler's *Water*, a typical canvas by this typically American artist. In such a work cubism becomes a thoroughly naturalized form of expression.

In spite of all the violent forces loosed by the Armory Show, forces that tended to weaken ties with established traditions and to fracture the world into kaleidoscopic patterns, a substantial number of painters have continued to represent the real world more or less as it appears to the eye—or rather to the mind's eye; for with due regard for the realities, each saw the world about him differently. Edward Hopper was such a realist. He was an admirer of Eakins, although he created his own laconic version of man's world. This is often stark and lonely, as in *Office in a Small City* (PL. 16), one of his most representative paintings, in which he defines his subject by means of walls of light and shadows.

Thomas Hart Benton of Missouri, John Steuart Curry of Kansas, and Grant Wood of Iowa have been labeled "re-

FIG. 67.
Midnight Ride of Paul Revere, by
Grant Wood (1892-1942), oil on
masonite, 30 by 40 inches, 1931.
Arthur Hoppock Hearn Fund, 51.117.

gionalists" because of their devotion to their own Midwestern
scene. All three reveal the persistent strain of realism in American painting—a form of homespun realism that they considered
a provincial revolt against "the general cultural inconsequences
of American art" as it emanated from New York and Paris. In
his *July Hay*, Benton conveys the nature of labor at harvest time
in a rhythmic pattern of human figures, waving fields, and,
prominently in the foreground, lush vegetation. Wood's *Midnight Ride of Paul Revere* (FIG. 67) takes us to a distant toy-town
New England, pictured in an aerial view. This artist has been
fairly termed the most self-consciously primitive of the trained
painters of his generation.

The more fluid, more emotional distortion of natural forms
and color practiced by the French fauves found a native Ameri-

can expression, and in fact became one of our major art forms. The rugged strength and solid structure of Marsden Hartley's *Lobster Fishermen* suggests that expressionism is less a definable style than a creative attitude. Hartley was a born colorist who long and stubbornly worked toward his own distinctive way of using his pigments freely and stylizing natural forms.

Milton Avery retained recognizable images in his work, but reduced them to depersonalized flat patterns of color outlined in sharp rhythmical contours. In *Swimmers and Sunbather*, painted in 1945, his human figures and the features of a landscape setting are abstracted into a simplified color composition recalling those that Matisse had introduced in France some years earlier.

During the last two generations many other artists represented in the Museum's collection have produced more or less realistic figural canvases that reflect different aspects of the American experience and reveal the variety of individual talents that have made American art as richly and creatively diversified as any in the world. Both a stark and moving commentary on death in the coal mines by Ben Shahn and a pitiful representation of blind beggars by Jacob Lawrence speak in individual accents of human and social justice or the lack of it—of the failure of civilization that seemed so freshly apparent in the 1930s and 1940s that the theme became dominant in American art.

In those same years and later, there were more benign commentaries on the American scene, here represented in works by such men as Kenneth Hayes Miller, Reginald Marsh, Adolph Dehn, Jack Levine, and many others of singular talent.

The meticulously realistic tempera paintings of Andrew Wyeth, such as his *Grape Vine*, are realized with such controlled, flawless technique that the subject and the mood appeal directly, almost without our awareness of the medium by which they are conveyed.

Watercolors and Drawings

Because of the fragile nature of the material, the Museum's impressive collection of works of art on paper will be shown on a rotating basis in a special gallery. Here from time to time will be displayed such outstanding watercolors as Homer's *Fishing*

FIG. 68.
Spanish Fountain, by John
Singer Sargent (1856-1925),
pencil and watercolor, 20⁹/₁₆ by
13⁷/₁₆ inches, 1912.
Purchase, Joseph Pulitzer Bequest, 1915
(15.142.6).

Boats–Key West and Sargent's *Spanish Fountain* (FIG. 68). Both men did some of their finest work in this medium, where their quick grasp of reality found an ideal expression. Of Homer's watercolors the visiting English dramatist and novelist Arnold Bennett wrote, "They thrilled; they were genuine America; there is nothing else like them." In recording informal subjects as suited his mood, Sargent found the medium a perfect outlet for his extraordinary virtuosity.

Drawings and sketches by such disparate artists as Copley, Cole, Kensett, and Eakins, among others, often provide an intimate glimpse of the artist's immediate response to a subject of his choosing before he worked it over into some finished form. Here we are at the very origin of artistic accomplishment.

PERIOD ROOMS AND
FURNITURE GALLERIES

In the area behind and beyond the façade of the old United States Branch Bank are a series of so-called period rooms whose woodwork and other architectural features have been removed or reproduced from early dwellings that once stood in various colonies and states along the Atlantic seaboard. These range in date from the late seventeenth century to the early decades of the nineteenth. (When the installations are completed in 1981 they will be supplemented by additional interiors from buildings dating from the second quarter of the nineteenth century to the first years of the twentieth.)

These interior elements, preserved from neglect and destruction, are installed in the American Wing so that they approximate their original appearance as closely as possible. Furniture and accessories have been chosen and arranged so that the period rooms reflect their original uses. Paint colors for walls and woodwork were selected from colors popular when the rooms were built.

Virtually all the fabrics used for upholstery and for bed and window hangings throughout the Wing are faithful reproductions of materials that were originally used for these purposes. This practical expedient makes it possible to provide a more accurate view of the furniture and rooms than could be achieved by using contemporary materials that have survived from the past. By and large, these are delicate dress fabrics which, while in themselves interesting documents, are not suitable for use as room furbishings. Furthermore, experience has proved that the deterioration of old fabrics causes continued and serious maintenance problems. A few rare pieces with their original woolen needlework or leather upholstery, whose beauty has been vigilantly preserved, are on exhibit. The drapery designs of bed and window hangings follow pictorial and other documentary sources from the various periods represented.

A greater variety of related furniture than can be accommodated in the period rooms themselves is displayed in adjoining galleries. The exhibits are arranged in a roughly chronological sequence, starting with the earliest examples on the third floor. On each floor an introductory gallery provides explanatory information, including floor plans, photographs, and other material, that will enhance the visitor's understanding of the main exhibits.

THIRD FLOOR
Early Colonial Period, 1630-1730

In considering the earliest of these exhibits it is helpful to recall that the colonists who settled at widely separated points along the eastern seaboard in the seventeenth century intended to build and furnish their new homes as nearly like those they had left overseas as their skills and the materials at hand would permit. Not long after the first strains of settlement in a strange and sometimes hostile wilderness were eased, they succeeded in providing for themselves dwellings, meetinghouses and churches, furniture, silver, and other necessities and conveniences that did not differ appreciably in character or quality from English and Continental models. These first immigrants were largely persons of modest origins and although the craftsmanship they could command was modest in pretension, it was by no means crude. They came mostly from small towns and rural villages that lingered in the fading glow of the Middle Ages. Their work thus reflected the late Gothic styles of northern Europe, mainly England, hardly touched by the advanced fashions of courts and capitals where the transforming influence of the Renaissance was increasingly felt throughout the seventeenth century. It reflected also a way of life rooted in old habits that barely comprehended the comforts, the conveniences, and the more specialized arrangements that were so soon to become as widely appreciated in America as they were in Europe. This advance toward a more modern concept of living and the changing styles by which it was accommodated can be traced in the later rooms and other exhibits of the American Wing.

Meetinghouse Gallery

By way of introduction to the surrounding rooms and their furnishings a representative group of furniture of the early colonial period has been assembled in a large central gallery on the top floor. The heavy, roughly hewn roof trusses of this room, resembling those of the great Gothic and Tudor halls of

FIG. 69.
Chest, Ipswich, Massachusetts,
red and white oak, 1660-1680.
Gift of Mrs. Russell Sage, 10.125.685.

England, are adapted from the Old Ship Meetinghouse at
Hingham, Massachusetts, built in 1681 and still serving its
congregation. The original timbers at Hingham span a hall
forty-five feet across, wider than the nave of any English Gothic
cathedral, and are a lasting witness to the traditional woodwork-
ing skills of early colonial craftsmen. Those skills are manifest
on a reduced scale and in varying ways in the several types of
furniture assembled under this oaken framework and in nearby
galleries.

The chest was one of the most typical forms of seventeenth-
century furniture, as indeed it had been in ages past. In addition
to serving as a storage place, it sometimes doubled as a seat and,
since it was portable, as a kind of luggage. Like virtually all case
furniture of this early period, chests were constructed of
straight elements solidly joined together at right angles in an
uncompromisingly rectangular shape. From the earliest days of
settlement distinctive local and regional differences appeared in
the designs applied to this basic form. The front of one example
shown here is covered with flat carvings combining late Tudor
and Jacobean motifs in a manner associated with the work of
William Searle and Thomas Dennis of Ipswich, Massachusetts
(FIG. 69).

What are commonly referred to as sunflower chests because

of the nature of their stylized floral carvings were fashioned exclusively in the Connecticut River Valley in the neighborhood of Wethersfield. Such pieces, as in the case of one with two drawers displayed in this gallery, are also decorated with applied split spindles and bosses stained black to simulate ebony. Still other regional variations in design can be attributed to the furniture makers of such separate centers as Hadley, Salem, Boston, and other Massachusetts towns and villages. A point to be made here is that these local differences, slight but clear indications of the diverse cultural strains that contributed to colonial society, continued to characterize American craftsmanship in the changing styles of years to come. This will be repeatedly demonstrated in the pages that follow.

The most highly developed seventeenth-century furniture form was the cupboard – the court cupboard and the press cupboard – used for the display of silver, pewter, brass, and pottery as well as for storage. In America such large and important pieces reached a peak of elaboration late in the century and then quickly went out of fashion. At the other extreme of size are miniature chests, cabinets, and boxes used for the storage of small objects which display the same type of carved and applied ornament as appears on the larger pieces (FIG. 70). In the central

FIG. 70.
Small cabinet, Massachusetts, Salem area, red oak, white pine, walnut, and maple, 1679.
Gift of Mrs. Russell Sage, 10.125.168.

gallery are also shown one of the earliest known American tables, consisting of trestles supporting a removable board, and a folding table with heavy turned legs, whose surface was at some time painted to simulate marble. The space-saving features of both were highly desirable for large families housed in small rooms.

A number of pieces in this gallery provide an introduction to the new standards of taste and style and the new forms that developed as the seventeenth century gave way to the eighteenth, a transition that will be explained in more detail in the discussion of other galleries and rooms. Such changes largely reflected the fashions that became popular in England during the reign of William and Mary, although in America what has come to be known as the William and Mary period of furniture design lasted long after the deaths of both those monarchs.

Among the new forms that were introduced during these years was the slant-top desk with drawers, a convenient successor to the primitive portable desk boxes that had served writers, after a fashion, since before the Middle Ages. A typical example is handsomely finished with highly figured veneers, a fashionable feature of much William and Mary cabinetwork that is also

FIG. 71.
Oval table, New England, maple, painted base, 1700-1730.
Gift of Mrs. Screven Lorillard, 52.195.4

displayed on a high chest of drawers (later to be known as a highboy), another innovative and convenient form of the period. A similar highboy, also with six legs connected by shaped stretchers, is decorated with japanning, a term coined to designate an inexpensive substitute for true oriental lacquer (PL. 18). Exotic figures in low relief, naïvely recalling Chinese and Japanese designs and taken from pattern books fancifully concocted in Europe, were modeled in gesso, covered with metal leaf, and varnished. The vogue for these decorative fantasies, produced for the most part by Boston craftsmen, endured until the middle of the eighteenth century.

Such pieces were provincial equivalents of stylish English models of some years earlier. Other contemporary forms evolved that had a decidedly native American character. With its scalloped skirt, neatly turned raking legs, and well-carved "Spanish" feet, a small maple table has a grace that owes little to the influence of foreign fashions (FIG. 71). Thus, too, a chest on frame or chamber table, a form that was probably an early type of dressing table, is painted with designs that are peculiar to the neighborhood of Guilford, Connecticut.

Hart Room

The room from the Thomas Hart house, built in Ipswich, Massachusetts, before 1674, is the earliest of the Museum's American rooms. Its massive fireplace lined with large irregular bricks suggests the size of the chimney pile around which the house was constructed. Hand-hewn oak corner posts, horizontal supports, or girts, and the huge, chamfered summer beam that spans the room from the chimney to the end wall of the house, frankly reveal the structural skeleton of the building. All are securely joined by mortise and tenon joints. Clay and sun-dried brick were used to fill the walls between the studs, as may be seen in one exposed section. Boards lightly molded at the joins sheathe the fireplace wall. Wrought-iron hinges of various designs support the boarded doors of the room. The small casement windows with their diamond-shaped leaded panes are facsimiles of the original. Such houses were poorly heated (the large fireplace opening sucked in copious drafts of cold air from the outside), inadequately ventilated, and badly lighted (window glass was costly and efficient lamps had yet

Hart Room

FIG. 72.
Cupboard, Massachusetts,
Plymouth area, oak, pine,
maple, cedar, partly painted,
1670-1700.

Gift of Mrs. Russell Sage, 10.125.48.

to be developed). They were nevertheless soundly constructed in accordance with centuries-old traditions.

The Hart room is furnished with seventeenth-century oak and pine furniture, mostly of Massachusetts origin, such as the court cupboard (FIG. 72) and carved chest. An oak chair table represents another space-saving form, one mentioned in Massachusetts inventories as early as 1644. There are also a rocking cradle (FIG. 73), a bed (of later date; no seventeenth-century American beds are known to exist), and miscellaneous other furniture. These, with the recessed bake oven and the variety of utensils in the fireplace area, suggest the multiple purposes of such a room and the crowded circumstances over which household activities had to prevail.

FIG. 73.
Cradle, eastern Massachusetts,
white oak, 1640-1680.

Gift of Mrs. Russell Sage, 10.125.672.

Wentworth Room

The new standards of taste and design that evolved in the William and Mary period are handsomely demonstrated in the chamber (an upstairs room) from the John Wentworth house built at Portsmouth, New Hampshire. The woodwork of this room dates from about 1700, and most of the furnishings are from the years just preceding and following that date. The main staircase of this house has been installed separately across the large central gallery of the third floor.

The chamber itself has a higher ceiling and is more spacious than the Hart room, and its architectural features are more formally and deliberately treated. Constructional elements—all of white pine here—still intrude into the room, but two of the corner posts are neatly boxed in, the girts are deeply and decoratively chamfered, and the ceiling joists are concealed by plaster. The two other corner posts are gunstock shaped, providing a substantial bearing for the crosswise girts.

The fireplace wall is covered by wide panels with heavy moldings. The fireplace opening is itself framed by a robust bolection (projecting) molding and capped by a boldly fashioned mantel, a convenient resting place for glass and earthenware objects. The bricks within the fireplace are laid in a

119

Wentworth Room

herringbone pattern copied from a surviving example of the period, another instance of the deliberate attention to decorative detail that increasingly characterized the architecture of this period. Double-hung sash windows with molded muntins were introduced into America very late in the seventeenth century and have remained a standard treatment. The windows

FIG. 74.

High chest of drawers, eastern Massachusetts, maple veneer, walnut banding, maple, walnut, 1700-1730.

Gift of Mrs. Screven Lorillard, 52.195.2.

are still relatively small, and have been fitted with draw curtains following a fashionable design of the period. These permit a maximum amount of daylight to enter when they are raised. Brass door hardware replaces the shapely wrought-iron fixtures seen in the Hart room.

Against this background the new fashions of the William and Mary period are appropriately represented. Oak furniture all but disappears, replaced by lighter forms made of walnut, maple, and similar hardwoods. A six-legged maple-veneered highboy, a slightly variant form of the typical example shown in the central gallery, is here seen in a contemporary setting (FIG. 74). The highboy is paired with a lowboy, or dressing table, a custom that became more or less conventional in this period and that persisted for years to come. A group of tall-back William and Mary chairs with cushions of matching fabric and trimming further indicate the sense of order and formality that was becoming a ruling principle in domestic arrangements. The combination of caned seats and backs with curved relief carving–at times elaborately conceived–on chair frames and stretchers reflects the influence on colonial design of both the European Continent and, indirectly, the Orient. These features are displayed again in a daybed with the back canted for added comfort, a novel form of the period and a prototype of what would later be commonly known as a chaise longue. A number of these pieces, including the daybed, are of English origin and clearly illustrate the influence of imported examples on colonial craftsmanship. During this period the wing chair, or easy chair as it was then called, was introduced to the Colonies, a contribution to solid seating comfort that has not been improved upon since.

Until well into the eighteenth century Turkey "carpitts" continued to be used as table rather than floor coverings–by those who could afford such imported luxuries. The typical example shown in this room is laid over a gateleg table, still another space-saving form which came into fashion during the William and Mary period. Its two large drop leaves, when raised, were supported by movable legs hinged to swing out from the fixed central frame. Such other imported items as looking glasses and brass wall clocks, as well as tin-glazed pottery from Holland and England (broadly referred to as delftware) (FIG. 75), became increasingly common household accessories. Chinese porce-

FIG. 75.
Earthenware posset pot, England, possibly Lambeth, c. 1687.

Gift of Mrs. Russell S. Carter, 46.64.15.

Seventeenth and Early Eighteenth Century Furniture Gallery

FIG. 76.
Leather chair, Massachusetts, Boston area, maple, oak, 1720-1750.

Gift of Mrs. Russell Sage, 10.125.698.

lains that found their way to the wealthier American homes and silver plate fashioned both at home and abroad, such as those shown here in accordance with early household inventories, testify to the growing affluence of colonial society.

Seventeenth and Early Eighteenth Century Furniture Gallery

The progression of furniture styles from the last decades of the seventeenth century through the first decades of the eighteenth and the influences that conditioned their design are succinctly demonstrated in an array of chairs assembled in a neighboring gallery. Seating furniture was by no means so comfortable as it later became. Seventeenth-century chairs made few concessions to the irregularities and shifting positions of the human body, which even the frequent addition of loose cushions did little to accommodate; straight-lined, firm, and often elaborately turned and carved, they did however impose upon the sitter a measure of dignity and importance. The turned Brewster chair, so called because Elder William Brewster of Plymouth Plantation is said to have owned one of this type; the massive slat-back chair; and the boxlike wainscot chair with its solid paneled back emphatically illustrate these points. Built-in upholstery, as in a rare survival shown here whose seat and half-back are covered with Turkeywork over marsh-grass stuffing (PL. 17), marks the simple beginnings of new standards of comfort—standards that were met with great success a few decades later in the special case of the easy chair. Stools, often referred to as "joyned" or joint stools, remained a common form of seating furniture in homes and taverns, as they had been from time out of mind. The relative scarcity of such pieces today suggests the hard use to which they must have been put.

The radical innovations in chair design introduced with the William and Mary style were readily adopted in the Colonies and elegant refinements were sometimes faithfully copied by local craftsmen. Often, however, new fashion was modified in relatively simple versions of sophisticated English models. As in provincial England, durable and more readily available leather was substituted for cane. Local rushes made serviceable and inexpensive seats, and split spindles, or banisters, served for backs. Banister-back chairs continued to be made throughout the eighteenth century. One of the last and most enduring of these colonial variations was a simple and handsome descendant of the William and Mary line known as the Boston chair (FIG. 76). Usually upholstered in leather with a comfortably scooped back, its maple frame often painted red or black, it remained popular throughout the Colonies until the Revolutionary era.

In towns and villages more or less remote from the main urban centers, aspects of William and Mary lingered on to merge with features from both earlier and later modes. The resultant vernacular expression often had a highly individual charm. A convincing example shown in this gallery is a handsome armchair of a type attributed to John Gaines of Portsmouth, New Hampshire. It combines a boldly turned front stretcher, Spanish feet, a neatly carved crest, and solid back splat in the Queen Anne manner.

Bowler Room

Another room on the third floor is built around the long paneled fireplace wall taken from the country house of the wealthy merchant Metcalf Bowler. Constructed in Portsmouth, near Newport, Rhode Island, around 1763, the house had woodwork which dimly but pleasantly recalls the formal patterns of Georgian England. A cornice molding projects over fluted pilasters and doors to provide a rhythmic spacing of breaks. Here we meet for the first time in the American Wing architectural features that ultimately stemmed from classical sources. These had been transmitted to English builders through Renaissance versions. Architectural manuals in turn provided colonial craftsmen with English interpretations of the Renaissance designs. Throughout the eighteenth century this classical spirit thrice-removed was a persistent influence on American architecture, both exterior and interior.

Chairs with splat backs and yoke-shaped top rails show variant ways in which colonial makers successfully combined elements of the Queen Anne style with lingering traces of the earlier William and Mary (FIG. 77). From early in the eighteenth century, tall cases were devised to protect the works of clocks from dust and dirt and to accommodate their long pendulums which, controlled by an anchor escapement, improved their accuracy. Such impressive timepieces were thus the joint product

FIG. 77.
Chair, eastern Massachusetts or New Hampshire, maple, ash, 1730-1750.
Rogers Fund, 44.29.

Hewlett Room

FIG. 78.
Looking glass, England, walnut veneer on spruce, 1700-1730.
Gift of Mrs. J. Insley Blair, 45.119.

of the cabinetmaker and the clockmaker, only very occasionally combined in one person. They retained this general appearance for a century or more.

Looking glasses were made larger (they were still imported for the most part) and more revealing with better glass; their frames assumed more decorative shapes that gave them new importance as household accessories (FIG. 78). A walnut William and Mary mixing table made in New England has a spirits-proof top of slate inset in a marquetry border, probably a Swiss import. Curtains at the sash windows are reproductions of Indian printed cotton, a type of fabric long admired in the Western world.

Hewlett Room

A room salvaged from the John Hewlett house, built at Woodbury, Long Island, about 1740-60, has Dutch tiles surrounding the fireplace opening. Next to the fireplace is a shell-carved "beaufett," or cupboard, for the display of pottery, glassware, and other useful and decorative accessories. This in turn is beside a closet in the rear of which a concealed panel once led to a secret stairway. Here also the woodwork reflects the influence of English manuals. The fluted pilasters that are carried up into projections of the cornice represent in provincial fashion a classical architectural entablature not clearly understood. In the Hart room the structural needs of the house, frankly stated, made the style. In this case the formalities of applied designs largely obscure the underlying framework of the house. The abbreviated pilasters over the fireplace, for example, rest on nothing and do not even suggest structural supports. The woodwork is painted in a blue based on the original color.

A painted cupboard, or kas, from the Hudson River area (FIG. 79), is a delightful reminder of the huge Dutch prototypes whose expensive woods and ornate carvings are here replaced by grisaille painted decoration. Such representations of fruit and vegetable forms could be considered the earliest examples of American still-life painting. A type of chair also characteristic of New York from Long Island to Albany ingenuously blends features of various early styles. Commonly painted, its solid back splat and pad feet recall Queen Anne fashions whereas its straight stiles, boldly turned front stretcher, and rush seat continue earlier traditions. Local craftsmen turned out such engagingly simple forms until the early 1800s. Another type of regional chair, this one identified with the Delaware River valley in New Jersey and Pennsylvania, has a tall back with six arched slats arranged in graduated sizes.

New York Alcove

The stained gumwood paneling of a fireplace wall from a stone house built in High Falls, Ulster County, New York, in 1752 is preserved in an alcove nearby. Once again, fluted pilasters and an elaborate cornice, ornamented with dentils, are reminders of the widespread influence of imported design books. The concave corners of the raised panel above the fireplace, similar to other examples to be seen in that general area, may represent the influence of Huguenot craftsmen known to have worked there.

FIG. 79.
Kas, New York, pine, oak, painted decoration, 1690-1720.
Gift of Sarah Elizabeth Jones, 23.171.

Wentworth Stair

The furniture assembled in this small gallery is largely of New York workmanship, including most prominently a gumwood high chest of drawers whose five spiral-turned legs and flat stretchers recall European styles of the period of Charles I and Charles II. An early gumwood desk on frame with turned legs and a shaped skirt accented with pendent drops is an unusual variant of New York cabinetwork (FIG. 80). An inscription under the lid, although unfortunately illegible, is certainly in the Dutch language and suggests that the desk was passed down from the family of an early Dutch settler. A drop-leaf, trestle-based table and a pair of leather-upholstered chairs are also of New York origin.

Wentworth Stair

The other exhibits on the third floor take us back to New England. The main staircase of the Wentworth house (FIG. 81), a rare survival, has been installed adjacent to the New York alcove. It is distinguished by unusual spiral-turned balusters and attractive molded paneling covering the chimney bricks.

FIG. 80.
Desk on frame, New York City, gumwood, walnut (?) veneer, 1695-1720.
Rogers Fund, 44.47.

FIG. 81.
Stair from the John Wentworth house, Portsmouth, New Hampshire, c. 1700.
Sage Fund, 26.290.

Newington Room

Originally, the stairs wound to the upper floor at a steep pitch from immediately within the front entrance of the house.

Newington Room

A paneled unfinished-pine fireplace wall from a house built in Newington, Connecticut, about the middle of the eighteenth century has fluted pilasters, arched panels, and a shell-top cupboard. Here the formal modes of the day have been translated discreetly and agreeably into a strictly native and local idiom. Rosettes carved in the "capitals" of the pilasters and crossed stiles in the lower wainscoting are both typical of eighteenth-century interiors of the Connecticut River valley.

FIG. 82.
Chest of drawers, Connecticut, Windsor area, yellow pine, maple, painted decoration, 1720–1750.
Gift of Mrs. J. Insley Blair, 45.78.3.

Sliding shutters at the windows, as here installed, were occasionally used in such houses as this woodwork came from. The butterfly table, a graceful and apparently a distinctively colonial variant of the drop-leaf, received its modern name from the shape of the solid "wings," or brackets, that swivel on the side stretchers and support the hinged leaves when they are raised. The outward raking legs, turned in the popular vase-and-ring design, add to the appealing character of this native form.

The difficulties of overland travel in colonial America made waterways—rivers and bays—the main arteries of communication. Along with freight and news, fashions and styles moved upstream to inland communities, to be adapted by country craftsmen to local taste, needs, and materials. Down to the present day, there has never been a time in American history when some forms of furniture were not painted either with flat color or in decorative patterns. By the early years of the eighteenth century, several distinctive styles of painted decoration were being practiced in various areas of Connecticut. At the mouth of the Connecticut River, in and near the little town of Guilford, chests of different types were painted with combinations of motifs in the British royal arms—fleurs-de-lis, roses, crowns, and thistles—intermingled with undulating vines, vase shapes, and stylized floral forms. Just what models may have been used for these designs—embroideries, formal patterns of wooden inlays on more sophisticated furniture, or heraldic devices—it is not possible to say.

Well up the Connecticut River valley in the area of Windsor, Connecticut, chests were decorated with a fanciful arrangement of human figures, dogs, butterflies, trees, flowers, and architectural silhouettes, all brightly delineated in a rather random pattern (FIG. 82).

Elsewhere in New England other types of painted designs were produced in certain regions. Among them is a group of chests apparently made by Robert Crossman, a drum maker of Taunton, Massachusetts, in the second quarter of the eighteenth century. These display delicately drawn designs combining birds, scrolling vines, flowers, and trees.

Hampton Room

A passage from the Newington room leads into a chamber from a farmhouse in Hampton, New Hampshire, a hamlet near

Hampton Room

the Massachusetts border. This little room has no fireplace; its walls and ceiling are completely paneled in unpainted pine. As could have been the case in the eighteenth century, a simple folding bed furnished with checked linen occupies one corner of the room. Country versions of fashionable furniture once again illustrate how pleasantly the current styles were simplified and adapted by the rural artisan and how older styles lingered on long after they had been abandoned in sophisticated circles. An unpretentious but trimly designed pine cupboard is a late descendant of the massive oak press cupboard of earlier times (FIG. 83). The slat-back chairs, also known as ladder-backs, are provincial New England versions of a traditional type that has been produced for centuries with various modifications.

FIG. 83.
Cupboard, New England, pine, maple, partly painted, 1710–1750.
Gift of Mrs. Russell Sage, 10.125.45.

SECOND FLOOR
Late Colonial Period, 1730-1790

One more superb example of the woodwork peculiar to the Connecticut River valley, a pedimented doorway from West-field, Massachusetts (FIG. 84), is installed at the south end of the second-floor introductory gallery. It demonstrates in a most engaging manner how effectively local craftsmen could trans-late the stately language of Renaissance architecture into a lively vernacular. The wooden frame of the doorway is regu-larly gouged and painted to simulate cut stone. But what were probably only dimly remembered fluted Corinthian pilasters of some original model have been converted into a spirited exer-cise in flat carving. The leafy tendrils that run up the pilasters and those that form the capitals are a purely local invention; the cushion frieze above the door and the scrolled pediment that surmounts the frame follow the contours of available molding planes. The outlines of the entire doorway are duplicated in miniature on the base of each pilaster in an ingenuous provincial pattern.

In the exhibits on this floor, the stylistic trends that suc-ceeded William and Mary and that were briefly referred to on the floor above develop profusely. The interiors and furniture largely date from the middle decades of the eighteenth century, a period culminating in the Revolutionary War. An increasing use of mahogany, along with handsomely grained black walnut, made for more opulent appearances. Curved lines become more suave and, as the late colonial period advanced, carving became more intricate and cut in higher relief. The Queen Anne style reached and passed a peak of popularity in this period and was gradually superseded by designs such as were featured in the pattern books of Thomas Chippendale, Robert Manwaring,

and their English contemporaries, manuals that were freely referred to throughout the Colonies.

The term "Chippendale style" is used loosely to describe much of the furniture made in the last decades of the colonial period, owing to the fame acquired over the years by *The Gentleman and Cabinet-Maker's Director.* Originally issued by Chippendale in 1754, and in an enlarged edition in 1762, this was the first fully illustrated manual devoted entirely to furniture. Many of his influential designs were adaptations of the French rococo style to the English taste. As in earlier years, different regions along the Atlantic coast evolved separate versions of the prevailing styles.

Alexandria Ballroom

The largest interior on this floor is the assembly room from Gadsby's Tavern in Alexandria, Virginia, once a major coach stop on the much traveled route between the northern cities and the southern plantations. Although the tavern was built in 1793, the architectural details of this room do not differ significantly from those of the other pre-Revolutionary rooms on the second floor, showing the persistent influence of the manuals published earlier in the century. In all these rooms, it will be noted that the designs specified in the imported guides are followed more literally and executed with better understanding of the principles involved than in the rooms earlier described; that is, the interpretations are more "correct." The two chimney breasts and the doors of the assembly room are surmounted by scrolled pediments; the walls are paneled only to the chair rails; and reproductions of Venetian blinds such as were advertised in a newspaper of 1767 are used at the curtained windows.

A little musicians' gallery hung high on the wall opposite the fireplaces recalls the festive occasions celebrated at the tavern. Here, in 1798, George Washington attended his last birthnight ball. Most appropriately, a mahogany spinet in the Queen Anne style (FIG. 85) is among the furnishings displayed in the ballroom. On a maple panel above the keyboard of this exceptional piece is the inscription "John Harris, Boston New England fecit." It is the earliest American work of Harris, immigrant member of a family of eminent London musical-instrument makers, and when he completed it and shipped it off

FIG. 84. (OPPOSITE) Doorway from a house in Westfield, Massachusetts.

Rogers Fund, 16.147.

to a Newport customer in 1769, the Boston press duly and proudly reported that this "very curious spinet" was "the first ever made in America." Actually, this distinction belongs to another spinet in the Museum's collection, made in 1739 by Johann Clemm of Philadelphia.

The basic elements of style are more immediately visible in chairs than in any other furniture form. The ample space of the ballroom provides an opportunity to display a variety of chairs that illustrate the late colonial styles—Queen Anne and Chippendale—as the first developed, then merged with the second in the course of the eighteenth century. With the introduction of Queen Anne every trace of Tudor and Puritan stiffness vanished. Every vestige of the elaborate ornamental scrolls, turnings, and pierced carvings of high-style William and Mary furniture gave way to undulating curved elements that both please the eye and serve the needs of solid construction. In this classic harmony of form and function, decorative carving played only a secondary role.

The single most conspicuous element of this graceful construction was the cabriole leg, an S-shaped support. Curves were repeated in serpentine stretchers, horseshoe-shaped seats, and rounded solid splats molded to the contours of the human spine and framed by rounded supporting stiles continuous with arched crest rails. At its best it was the most satisfactory expression in colonial furniture design. Queen Anne chairs were still

FIG. 85.
Bentside spinet, by John Harris (active 1730-1769), Boston, mahogany, mahogany veneer, 1769.

Purchase, Anonymous Gift, Friends of the American Wing Fund, Sansbury-Mills, Dodge, and Pfeiffer Funds, and funds from various donors, 1976.229.

FIG. 86.
Armchair, Philadelphia, wal-
nut, 1740-1760.
Rogers Fund, 25.115.36.

being made in America more than two generations after that monarch's death in 1714. The neighborhoods of Boston, New-port, New York, Philadelphia, and various other areas of the country each had its distinctive interpretation of the style. Those made in Philadelphia during the middle years of the century, some departing into Chippendale flourishes, are among the most graceful achievements of colonial craftsman-ship (FIG. 86). A walnut settee of Queen Anne design with scrolled cresting and curved arms descended in the family of James Logan, William Penn's secretary and the builder of a handsome mansion called Stenton.

By the middle of the eighteenth century the relatively quiet curves of the Queen Anne style were gradually being sup-planted by more exuberant designs, such as those recom-mended by Chippendale in his *Director*. There were two main factors in the change: the increasing use of mahogany, a worm-resistant wood that is almost as strong as metal and can be carved in the most intricate patterns; and the prevalence of the new manuals published with the working properties of mahogany clearly in mind specifically for the guidance of furniture makers. Regional variations were as many and as marked as they had been earlier. In the decades preceding the Revolution the most ambitious furniture was produced in Philadelphia, then the most progressive and populous of colonial cities. Country craftsmen in small towns, villages, and rural farming areas turned out simplified versions in local woods. In either case, square seat frames, pierced back splats, bow-shaped cresting rails, and cabriole legs with claw-and-ball feet were the main distinguishing features of the style. Oddly, the cabriole leg with claw-and-ball foot, considered almost a hallmark of colonial furniture in the Chippendale style, is virtually ignored in the *Director*.

In the assembly room as in other rooms on this floor, higher ceilings made it possible and practical to install chandeliers. The pair of twelve-light brass examples here are of a kind imported from England for lighting churches and public buildings. The excellence of native brass workers is well demonstrated by two sets of andirons in a pattern associated with the foundry work of Paul Revere and his son. Thanks to technical advances in glassmaking, looking glasses, whose frames shared the contemporary spirit of architectural design in their moldings and scroll pediments, grew larger and increased the illumination of rooms with their abundant reflections of candlelight.

New England Furniture Gallery

In a central gallery adjoining the ballroom, a variety of chairs and case pieces trace the flowering of the Queen Anne and Chippendale styles in and about Boston. Generally speaking, lean proportions and restrained ornamentation are characteristic of furniture made in Massachusetts. The relatively slender legs and narrow backs of chairs are typical features of both styles. A walnut-veneered and inlaid highboy (FIG. 87) and matching lowboy with carved and gilded shell ornament are supported by slim, delicately shaped cabriole legs terminating in pad feet. The broken-scroll pediment of the highboy, its fluted pilasters, and its three corkscrew finials add to the importance of this rare pair as examples of the highly developed Queen Anne style as it was realized in Boston in the second quarter of the eighteenth century.

FIG. 87.
High chest of drawers, Boston,
walnut, walnut veneer, 1730–
1760.
Gift of Mrs. Russell Sage, 10.125.62.

Almodington Room

Many of the fine case pieces made in Massachusetts in the decades immediately preceding the Revolution were of block-front construction. Blocking, in which a flattened concave central section on the front of a piece is flanked by two convex sections, was by no means restricted to Massachusetts cabinetwork, but it was apparently first practiced in that colony and enjoyed a long popularity there. (It is worth noting that this feature rarely occurs in English furniture.) The excellent examples shown in this gallery include several desks and secretaries. One of the latter, distinguished by crisply carved scallop shells on the skirt and top, by perfect proportions, and by a lustrous glowing patina, bears the enigmatic inscription "Nath Gould not his work." Gould died in 1781, the richest cabinetmaker in Salem. Did a disgruntled employee record for posterity that this masterful desk was his work, not that of his employer?

In the case of another secretary, the lower carcass swells out from top to bottom on the front and both sides, in what is called a bombé form. Sometimes known also as a kettle base because it curves in a bulging kettle shape, this opulent design was especially well understood and executed by craftsmen of the Boston area. The attractively paneled doors of the upper case have delicately carved moldings and are flanked by fluted pilasters topped by unusual capitals. The doors open onto an arrangement of well-designed cubbyholes, shelves, and drawers which are supplemented by others behind the slanting desk front.

An especially interesting provincial version of the block-front, a slant-top desk of cherry wood, was made at Colchester, Connecticut, by Benjamin Burnham. The inscription on the desk, stating that Burnham had "sarved his time in Felledlfey," is a quaint reminder of the itinerant habits of many colonial craftsmen. So exuberant was Burnham's three-tiered bank of robustly curved interior drawers that in the end he had to cut niches out of the lid so that it would close over the drawers.

FIG. 88. (OPPOSITE)
Bedstead post, Massachusetts, mahogany, 1760-1790.
Gift of Mrs. Russell Sage, 10.125.336.

Almodington Room

New England furniture was often shipped to the southern colonies, and examples have been installed in a room adjoining the central gallery taken from a brick house known as Almodington in Somerset County, Maryland. The walls of this interior, divided horizontally by a heavy chair rail, are paneled from floor to ceiling in a manner that was gradually going out of fashion by the middle of the eighteenth century. The present mantelpiece replaced an earlier one about 1800. In the shell-top cupboards on either side of the fireplace might have been arranged Delftware from Holland, salt-glazed pottery from England, and possibly China Trade porcelains, all of which added decorative emphasis to many rooms of the time.

The room is furnished as a gentleman's bedroom. The most conspicuous piece in it is a Boston-made four-poster bed with cabriole front legs that have detachable carved kneecaps and that terminate in boldly shaped claw-and-ball feet (FIG. 88). The bed hangings and the upholstery on an attendant easy chair and a suite of side chairs—also made in Boston—are all cut from the same cloth. This is raspberry red wool moreen in a Vermicelli pattern in winter, and a green-and-white cotton check in summer, both exact reproductions from eighteenth-century samples. As often as not a single fabric, or hue at least, served throughout a room as it does here, and as contemporary references to "the red room," for example, or "the green room" indicate. Appropriately, a dressing table and a shaving mirror stand between the windows. A highboy or a chest-on-chest served for the storage of wearing apparel, linens, and so forth, in a day when closets were not yet common conveniences.

Powel Parlor

A parlor from Samuel Powel's house built about 1765 in Philadelphia incorporates a rich display of academic ornamental design drawn from contemporary English pattern books—a culmination of the advanced stylistic trends represented on this floor. The widely traveled Powel, last colonial mayor of the city, was host to George Washington, John Adams, and other prominent contemporaries. He was abreast of the latest fashions from abroad and wealthy enough to command the finest craftsmanship in furnishing and decorating his elegant town house. The carved and molded decoration of the wood-and-plaster-work are masterly interpretations of the style broadly associated with Chippendale's adaptations of the French rococo. The carving on the overmantel resembles that which distinguishes Philadelphia furniture of the period.

The plaster relief of the ceiling, in a design of swags of flowers, musical trophies, and pendant masks in the French manner, is a cast taken from the ceiling of the room adjoining

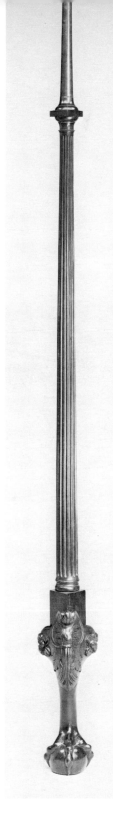

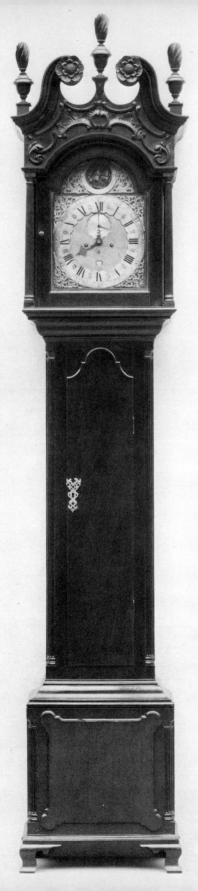

this one in the Powel house. The Chinese wallpaper, originally in another house of the same period, is a reminder of the oriental contribution to Western decoration in the eighteenth century. English porcelain statuettes on the mantelpiece, "burnt images and figures for mantlepieces," as they were described at the time, include one of John Wilkes, whose outspoken sympathy in the British Parliament for the American cause won him the gratitude of colonial patriots. The brass-and-iron fire grate was probably made in the Colonies. By the middle of the century wood for fire was occasionally in short supply in some urban areas and, as one contemporary observed, coal was being increasingly used "both for kitchen fires and in other rooms."

All the furniture in the Powel room is fashioned in the sophisticated version of the Chippendale style that was popular among the gentry of Philadelphia and its environs. Between the two windows a tall elaborately framed pier glass with gilded carving is hung above a side table. A number of side and armchairs with carved splats of varying popular patterns complement a tripod tilt-top table and smaller tripod stand, both supported by carved cabriole legs and generally used in the service of tea. A tall clock with scrolled pediment (FIG. 89) and a handsome mahogany desk further contribute to the elegance that so deeply impressed John Adams when he first visited the homes of Philadelphians on the eve of the Revolution.

Pennsylvania German Room

During those years when the master craftsmen of Philadelphia were producing such distinguished furnishings, German-speaking immigrants from the Rhine Valley and the Palatinate, who had been settling in the southeastern counties of Pennsylvania, were turning out totally different simple and colorful forms that harked back to old traditions of their homeland. The earliest of these settlers came to the New World in response to William Penn's offer of a refuge from persecution and hardship, and later they came in growing numbers as Penn's promises were abundantly fulfilled.

An exhibition gallery adjoining the Powel room displays a representative sampling of the work created by these earnest, religious, and industrious folk. The painted dower chests of the

Pennsylvania Germans, their cupboards and boxes, sgraffito and slipware pottery, objects in wrought iron, textiles, and illuminated writing or "fraktur" recall German prototypes but do not lack originality. The main feature of the gallery is a painted overmantel and chimneypiece from a house built about 1761 near Morgantown in Lancaster County (FIG. 90). The landscape in the overmantel panel was probably painted by some itinerant artist. The view was taken from an engraving after a Dutch painting reproduced in a book published at London in 1685.

FIG. 89. (OPPOSITE)
Tall clock, works by William Huston (active 1754-1771), Philadelphia, mahogany, 1767-1771.
Morris K. Jesup Fund, 48.99.

FIG. 90.
Painted overmantel panel from the Pennsylvania German room, Morgantown, Lancaster County, Pennsylvania; the landscape was copied from William Salmon's *Polygraphice*. . . . (London, 1685), c. 1761.
Morris K. Jesup Fund, 34.27.1,2,10.

A large open dresser, or cupboard, resting on trestle feet, its shelves lined with a variety of locally made earthenware, suggests the ample living these people reaped from the rich soil they so shrewdly selected for their farms and so zealously cultivated. The trestle table is a direct if distant descendant of medieval North European forms. A dower chest decorated with brightly painted floral or geometrical motifs is altogether typical of the heritage these people carried with them from overseas, and of the homely skills with which local artisans enlivened even the most commonplace accessories of daily living.

Van Rensselaer Hall

The area devoted to the late colonial period continues at a slightly higher level of this floor in a series of interiors and galleries where the regional characteristics of both furniture and architecture are demonstrated further and with special emphasis. Three interiors are of exceptional interest. A magnificent entry hall comes from the Van Rensselaer manor house, built at Albany, New York, between 1765 and 1769 by Stephen Van Rensselaer, the last patroon of that lordly domain. The house was one of the most important examples of Georgian architecture in the Middle Atlantic colonies. Originally the hall ran from front to rear entrance, with a stairway reached through an arch at one side. The intricate rococo carving in the spandrels of the archway is derived from an English design book of 1752.

The most remarkable feature of this impressively spacious passage is the scenic paper painted in England in 1768 especially for these walls. Its landscapes and seascapes, done in tempera after engravings of popular eighteenth-century European paintings, are surrounded by fanciful scrolls and rococo designs (FIG. 91). This large, high-ceilinged, and extravagantly decorated central room offers a spectacular contrast to the tiny entrance halls of earlier colonial dwellings.

All the furniture shown in the Van Rensselaer hall was made by New York craftsmen in the Chippendale style. A number of chairs with "ruffle and tassel" backs, gadrooned skirting, boldly fashioned claw-and-ball feet, and flat leaf carving—all characteristics of New York workmanship—were once owned by the Van Rensselaer family and may well have originally been used in this hall. An upholstered settee, made between 1757 and 1760, bears the label of Joseph Cox, upholsterer from London whose New York shop was then at the Sign of the Royal Bed in Dock Street. Two pier tables with thick marble tops and stout cabriole legs, and other chairs and tables, including a Van Rensselaer family card table, are also characteristic of the fine New York furniture produced in the years leading up to the Revolution.

FIG. 91. (OPPOSITE)
Wallpaper, English, detail depicting Winter, after Nicholas Lancret, from Van Rensselaer hall, Albany, New York, 1765-1769.
Gift of Dr. Howard Van Rensselaer, 28.224.

Verplanck Room

Still other examples of New York furniture of the period are shown in a parlor opening off the Van Rensselaer hall. By rare good fortune all the furnishings have been reassembled from their original home, the eighteenth-century residence of Samuel and Judith Crommelin Verplanck that stood at 3 Wall Street, New York City. This house was long ago demolished. A proper setting for the Verplanck furnishings has been provided by a room from another house of comparable date, built in Orange County by Cadwallader Colden, Lieutenant Governor of colonial New York.

Judging from the uniformity in style of these pieces it seems likely that most of them, particularly the card table (FIG. 92), settee, and set of six chairs—all with similarly designed legs—came from the shop of the same local maker. Two obvious exceptions, a red-and-gold japanned secretary and a gilt-framed Chinese Chippendale looking glass, were imported from England.

As may be seen in the cupboards flanking the fireplace, the

FIG. 92.
Card table, New York City, mahogany and mahogany veneer, 1760-1765.

Gift of James De Lancey Verplanck and John Bayard Rodgers Verplanck, 39.184.12.

Verplancks owned a complement of Chinese-export porcelain, a coveted ware that was brought to America via England and the Continent in growing quantities as the eighteenth century advanced. Several family portraits are by John Singleton Copley, colonial America's finest artist, who traveled up and down the Atlantic seaboard in search of commissions from well-to-do patrons. He observed of the New York gentry that they were so discerning he could "slight nothing" in taking their likenesses.

Marmion Room

One of the most interesting of all surviving early American domestic interiors is that from Marmion, the Virginia plantation home of the Fitzhugh family. Here the architectural treatment of Ionic pilasters and entablature conforms with unusual fidelity to the Renaissance conception of the classical orders. Part of the woodwork is painted to simulate marble; and on the larger wall panels landscapes suggestive of Dutch paintings, representations of urns with flowers, festoons of leaves, and asymmetrical scrolls are pleasantly composed. The corner fireplace opening is lined with its original Siena marble (FIG. 93); above it will hang the gilt-gesso rococo looking glass that always has hung in this room.

TWO LONG exhibition galleries take up the remaining space on this level. They are devoted to the display of selected examples of furniture made during the late colonial period in several different style centers. In these galleries it is possible to exhibit together a greater diversity of forms than could be appropriately combined in the period interiors—and once again regional variations in design and workmanship claim special attention.

Philadelphia Chippendale Furniture Gallery

In the Chippendale period the high chest of drawers, or highboy, reached its ultimate and most elaborate development. Predominant among these are the towering examples of Philadelphia, often with matching lowboys. Master carvers ornamented them with pierced shells, scrolling leaves, flowers, vines, and other naturalistic details in the rococo spirit of the

day. There are no English equivalents of such extreme treatment of the form.

The artistic quality and disposition of carved elements of the "Pompadour" highboy and its companion lowboy make them unsurpassed examples of eighteenth-century Philadelphia cabinetwork. The Pompadour highboy is so called because the roundly modeled bust in its scrolled pediment recalled to some imaginative mind the celebrated mistress of Louis XV. Other carved details on the drawer fronts were taken from designs published by Thomas Johnson, a contemporary English rococo furniture maker, and were apparently based on such fables as those of La Fontaine.

Another exceptional Philadelphia case piece, a chest on chest made 1770-1775 (PL. 19), is thought to be the joint work of two of the city's most prominent craftsmen: Thomas Affleck, cabinetmaker, and James Reynolds, carver. With its fluted quarter-columns, dentil fret, and broken-scroll pediment, the piece clearly reflects the influence of contemporary architectural manuals on furniture design. Like the Pompadour bust, the fantastic winged creature that seems to be rising from its perch on a combination of C-scrolls could be properly considered among the earliest examples of American sculpture in the round.

The virtuosity evident in these various examples of Philadelphia cabinetwork is also brilliantly demonstrated in the chairs, tables, and other forms fashioned in that populous and flourishing city, then the most eminent urban center in the British colonial world. Two pieces call special attention to the French influences that helped shape fashionable styles of the day. The first is a mahogany pier table with a marble top and unusually elaborate carving, whose four cabriole legs terminate in what are sometimes called French scroll feet. The second is a looking glass whose gilded frame consists of an exuberant combination of C-scrolls and other intricately carved rococo ornament.

The table once stood in the home of John Cadwalader, one of the most richly furnished dwellings in pre-Revolutionary Philadelphia. Easily one of the finest examples of seating furniture to have been produced in the Colonies is a remarkable side chair, also once owned by the Cadwaladers, which has ample proportions, a saddle-shaped seat, scalloped skirts, and hairy-paw front feet (FIG. 94). Like the superb linen press, still

FIG. 93. (OPPOSITE)
Detail of parlor fireplace wall, Marmion, King George County, Virginia, paneled c. 1735-1770, painted 1770-1780.
Rogers Fund, 16.112.

FIG. 94.
Side chair, attributed to Thomas Affleck (1740-1795), Philadelphia, mahogany, c. 1770.

Purchase, Sansbury-Mills and Rogers Funds, Emily C. Chadbourne Gift, Virginia Groomes Gift, in memory of Mary W. Groomes, Mr. and Mrs. Marshall P. Blankarn, John Bierwirth and Robert G. Goelet Gifts, The Sylmaris Collection, Gift of George Coe Graves, by exchange, Gift of Mrs. Russell Sage, by exchange, and funds from various donors, 1974.325.

FIG. 95.
Desk and bookcase, Newport,
Rhode Island, mahogany,
1760–1790.
Rogers Fund, 15.21.2.

another Cadwalader piece shown here, its design is strictly English. But it was made locally at a time when imports of fashionable London furniture were being boycotted by patriotic colonists.

A singularly handsome tripod table has a scalloped, or pie-crust, edge made of one piece of mahogany. The tabletop, which spins freely when in use and tilts up when the table is put aside, is supported by a fluted column rising from boldly shaped carved cabriole legs whose terminal claws tensely clutch ball feet. The rest of the exhibits, an easy chair, a pole screen with hairy-paw feet, and a Pembroke table among them, amplify the impression of opulence and supreme craftsmanship typical of Philadelphia furniture at its best.

Eighteenth Century Furniture and Decorative Arts Gallery

A totally different, more restrained but hardly less sophisticated style of the same period was peculiar to the area in and about the little seaport of Newport, Rhode Island. The most prominent feature of this style was the blockfronts of case pieces, with their alternately raised and recessed panels surmounted by carved convex and concave shells of a highly distinctive character. Neither blockfront furniture nor carved shells were peculiar to colonial Rhode Island, but nowhere else were these two elements more successfully integrated into a distinctive organic pattern. The blocking, usually carved from the solid wood, extends from shaped panels in the pediments of tall pieces down through the door and drawer fronts, through the moldings and even into the bracket-shaped feet, where they are accented by delicately carved scrolls. These points are well illustrated by a tall secretary with six shells and a closed bonnet top (FIG. 95). In these and certain other distinguishing features, colonial Rhode Island cabinetwork owes nothing either to Chippendale or to any other contemporary English designers whose works were known in America.

Most of the prime surviving examples of such furniture were produced by one or another of the members of the interrelated Goddard and Townsend families, several of whose signed and labeled pieces are exhibited here. Among them are a chest of drawers and a tall-case clock, both made by John Townsend in

149

the 1760s. Although they are by craftsmen as yet unidentified, a card table and a marble-topped pier table also display features peculiar to the Newport area: sharply contoured cabriole legs, more square than rounded in section and carved in a unique combination of cameo and intaglio designs of leafage in almost geometric patterns; and ball-and-claw feet with the slender talons undercut to leave open spaces between claw and ball. The last was a refinement sometimes practiced in England but not elsewhere in the Colonies.

One exceptional piece, a marble-topped commode, or bureau, with a serpentine front (FIG. 96), follows a design markedly different from any of the others—more French than Anglo-American in spirit. It is attributed to John Goddard. Another most unusual piece, an easy chair in the Queen Anne style, retains its original upholstery. The front and sides are covered with fine bargello needlepoint and the back with a colorful landscape worked in crewel. The chair is unique in being signed and dated by the upholsterer, "Gardner, Jr. Newport 1758."

Japanned pieces are gathered in one alcove of this exhibition area. As earlier noted, the rather tricky art of japanning seems to have been practiced mainly but not solely in Boston. Because

FIG. 96.
Chest of drawers, Newport, Rhode Island, mahogany, marble, 1750-1790.

Purchase, Emily C. Chadbourne Bequest, Gifts of Mrs. J. Amory Haskell and Mrs. Russell Sage, by exchange, and The Sylmaris Collection, Gift of George Coe Graves, by exchange, 1972.130.

FIG. 97.
High chest of drawers, Boston,
maple, japanned, 1747.
Gift of Mrs. Russell Sage, 10.125.58.

of the fragile nature of its built-up surfaces, furniture with this
sort of whimsical and exotic decoration has survived in relatively small numbers. It is therefore an unusual circumstance
that, besides the earlier highboy shown on the third floor, the
Museum can here display two japanned highboys (FIG. 97) with
matching lowboys in the Queen Anne style. These rare pieces,
with their odd combination of carved and gilded shells and
classical architectural motifs and their pseudo-oriental ornamental designs—all applied to typically regional forms—provide

151

a singular witness to the crosscurrents of interest and taste that contributed to the pattern of life in colonial America.

Before the fashion for japanning waned around the middle of the eighteenth century, the technique was apparently applied to virtually all forms of furniture. Also shown in this alcove are a looking glass and a shaving glass, the latter having been imported from England by the owner of the dressing table on which it stands.

In addition to the numerous clocks shown elsewhere in the American Wing a group of representative examples made in the various colonies has been brought together here. These are for the most part tall-case clocks (FIG. 98) and the cabinetwork enclosing the works reflects the general development of styles as well as the regional preferences in design and detail of craftsmen from Boston, Newport, Connecticut, and Philadelphia. (The term "grandfather clock" was derived from a popular song of the 1880s.) Tall clocks were costly and toward the end of the colonial period smaller and somewhat less expensive shelf and wall clocks, some driven by springs rather than weights, were produced at a number of shops.

FIG. 98.

Tall clock, works by Benjamin Willard (1743-1803) and Simon Willard (1754-1849), Roxbury, Massachusetts, mahogany, 1772.

Gift of Dr. and Mrs. Brooks H. Marsh, 1976.341.

PLATE 19. (RIGHT)

Chest on chest, Philadelphia, mahogany, mahogany veneer, 1770-1775.

Purchase, Friends of the American Wing and Rogers Funds, Virginia Groomes Gift, in memory of Mary W. Groomes, Mr. and Mrs. Frederick M. Danzinger, Hermanann Merkin and Anonymous Gifts, 1975.91.

PLATE 20.

Pier table, by Joseph B. Barry & Son (active 1794-d. 1838), Philadelphia, mahogany with gilt-bronze mounts, c. 1815.

Purchase, Friends of the American Wing Fund, Anonymous Gift, George M. Kaufman Gift, Sansbury-Mills Fund, and Gift of Mrs. Russell Sage, Gift of the Members of the Committee of the Bertha King Benkard Memorial Fund, John Stewart Kennedy Fund, Bequest of Martha S. Tiedeman, Gift of Mrs. Frederick Wildman, Gift of F. Ethel Wickham, Gift of Edgar William and Bernice Chrysler Garbisch, Gift of Mrs. F. M. Townsend and Bequest of W. Gedney Beatty, by exchange, 1976.324.

FIRST FLOOR
Early Federal Period, 1790-1820

The material exhibited on the first floor dates from the several decades following the Revolutionary War, years that are broadly referred to as the Federal period. With the end of hostilities, fresh currents of taste and design flowed into the new republic from European countries, notably England and France. A second classical revival was taking place, this time based not on Renaissance concepts as in the earlier Georgian period, but on a more direct and accurate knowledge of ancient art and architecture. Among other remains that were scattered throughout the Mediterranean world and accessible for study by archaeologically-minded adventurers were the recently excavated ruins of Pompeii and Herculaneum. Suddenly buried (and preserved) by volcanic ash in the first century A.D., these cities provided a whole new vocabulary of ornament and decoration which was translated into the Louis XVI style in France and its equivalent in England.

The foremost exponents of neoclassical fashions in England were the Scottish architect-designers Robert and James Adam. Their *Works in Architecture*, published at London in 1773-1779, had an electric effect on the development of both architecture and the decorative arts. The impact of these books by the Adam brothers was very soon reflected in the plates of other English books on furniture design produced by Thomas Shearer, George Hepplewhite, and Thomas Sheraton. In these manuals, elegant Adam designs were modified so that it was practical to offer them to a wider public.

As promulgated by such pattern books, which quickly reached America, the new style was at once dignified and ostensibly simple. The robust exuberance of the Chippendale style with its asymmetrical and eclectic accents gave way to lighter forms of measured symmetry and delicate grace. Carving was subdued in favor of inlay and veneer arranged in simple geometric patterns. Along with the development of the new style, there evolved different types of furniture designed to further the comforts and conveniences of life—sideboards, washstands, wine coolers, sewing tables, bookcases, and other household appurtenances that had earlier played little or no part in the domestic routine.

In fashionable houses of the Federal period, rooms tended to be more spacious than formerly, with higher ceilings and larger windows (which sometimes extended, French style, even to the floor). Oval, round, and octagonal rooms added variety to floor plans. By the end of the eighteenth century, the up-to-date American home might have had numerous rooms for special purposes—a dining room, a parlor, a library, a ballroom, as well as a kitchen and bedrooms (but rarely a bathroom)—creating an environment far removed from that of the all-purpose seventeenth-century hall.

Federal Gallery

The doorway of the façade of the United States Branch Bank, built in 1822-1824, leads from the courtyard into a large exhibition gallery displaying distinguished examples of furniture from the Federal period. Antique elements from a Baltimore Federal house and reproductions from other American buildings of the period have been combined to produce the architectural trim of the gallery—delicately detailed and slenderly proportioned cornice and door surrounds.

These first-floor galleries demonstrate that regional characteristics in furniture became even more pronounced after the Revolution. A large banquet board shown in the center of this area, for example, is an impressive example of typical New York workmanship. It is composed of three separate divisions, each with four-column platform supports and gracefully outsweeping legs with carved knees.

The styles popularized by Sheraton and Hepplewhite were introduced into this country not only by the publications of those designers, but by immigrant craftsmen who came here with some training and experience. They brought with them or here developed their own personal interpretation of the prevailing styles. The suave curves of the banquet board, and the skilled disposition of a few decorative elements of carving and turning are features associated with the work of the Scotch immigrant Duncan Phyfe. His superior craftsmanship and individual versions of English styles were in his own lifetime hailed far beyond the environs of New York. Similar features are seen in the matching chairs from an original set of twenty-four with lyre backs and front feet carved in the shape of paws—both fashionable motifs based on ancient models.

Also typical of New York's version of the English Regency style, and also possibly from Phyfe's celebrated shop, are a pair of unusual marble-topped consoles, or pier tables. Turned, reeded, and carved legs—all four terminating in massive paw feet—and brass-trimmed apron edges distinguish the tables. These handsome pieces originally graced the home of Moses Rogers, one of New York's finest Federal houses, at 7 State Street across from the Battery. An extraordinary worktable, unique alike in its design and its intricately and ingeniously constructed interior, may also well have been a product of the versatile and accomplished Phyfe.

Craftsmen both north and south of New York continued to interpret the prevailing styles in ways peculiar to their separate regions. While derived ultimately from a plate in Sheraton's *Dictionary* (where it is termed the "Sister's Cylinder Bookcase,") the design of a large, elaborate, and colorful desk and bookcase has been artfully and originally worked in a manner that identifies it with Baltimore or Philadelphia. The inlaid satinwood ovals and banding and, more conspicuously, the two flanking panels of glass with neoclassical painted decorations, are devices that have in the past been particularly associated with Baltimore Federal furniture. An attribution to that lively port city is fortified by a penciled inscription on the bottom of one of the drawers noting the marriage of Margaret Oliver of Baltimore to Roswell Lyman Colt on October 5, 1811.

Another elaborate piece of furniture from the same general area and period, a pier table, combines almost the entire vocabulary of the skilled cabinetmaker's methods of decoration in its veneered panels, carving, gilding, and ormolu mounts (PL. 20). Made by the Irish immigrant Joseph B. Barry and his son at their Philadelphia cabinetmaker's shop, it reveals the influence of Sheraton's designs in carved and pierced decoration on its back gallery. The griffin motif, popular in Baltimore at this

Philadelphia Gallery

time, is here associated with garlands twining around the columns in the French fashion.

A sideboard that was probably made in the workshop of Thomas Seymour of Boston (FIG. 99) offers a distinctly different variation of the Sheraton style. Sideboards were introduced to America during the Federal period as dining rooms assumed an increasingly important role in social life. They became, in the words of Robert Adam, "apartments of conversation." Notable characteristics of this Boston-made example are tambour doors ("Shutters," as they were called by Sheraton) with alternating dark and light strips, urn-shaped ivory escutcheons, brass lion's-head drawer pulls, and sensitive reeding and carving on posts and legs.

Philadelphia Gallery

The special distinction of Philadelphia neoclassical furniture can be seen in an adjoining gallery where a number of highly representative examples are concentrated. An eight-foot-tall secretary presents a brilliant arrangement of mirrored panels and satinwood and mahogany veneers on door and drawer fronts. Concealed in the satinwood interior are neatly and

FIG. 99.
Sideboard, attributed to the workshop of Thomas Seymour (active 1794-1843), Boston, mahogany, mahogany and birch veneers, birch, cherry, and holly inlays, 1805-1815.

Gift of the family of Mr. and Mrs. Andrew Varick Stout, in their memory, 65.188.1.

conveniently disposed bookshelves, pigeonholes, drawers, and an adjustable writing surface. With justifiable pride, John Davey inscribed his name seven times on inconspicuous surfaces to establish his authorship of this secretary. It remains the only known documented example of his craftsmanship. Although more massive, another desk and bookcase made in Philadelphia shows equal attention to refined detail (FIG. 100).

FIG. 100.
Gentleman's secretary, Philadelphia, mahogany veneer, mahogany and satinwood inlay, painted polychrome decoration, 1795-1805.

Purchase, Joseph Pulitzer Bequest, 1967 (67.203).

Made about 1790, it is decorated with carefully disposed veneers, intricate inlays, and polychrome painted designs. This
extremely impressive case piece was apparently ordered from
some unidentified cabinetmaker by Maskell Ewing, Jr., whose
name is inscribed on a drawer.

Chairs in the gallery represent Philadelphia variations of
Sheraton and Hepplewhite designs. Except for minor details,
square-back chairs made by Henry Connelly and Ephraim
Haines are virtually identical local adaptations of the Sheraton
style. At one time or another both men supplied furniture to the
French-born Stephen Girard, merchant, financier, philan-
thropist, and distinguished Philadelphia citizen. A pair of exceptional painted chairs with open oval backs framing six
curved plumes and other decorative motifs, generally patterned
after a design in Hepplewhite's *Guide*, were probably also made
in Philadelphia for a member of the prominent Derby family of
Salem, Massachusetts (FIG. 101). It is certain at least that in 1796
the wealthy Salem merchant Elias Hasket Derby ordered two
dozen chairs of similar design from Philadelphia; these could
have been part of that shipment.

Haverhill Room

The woodwork of the interior adjacent to the Philadelphia
gallery comes from the Duncan house, built in Haverhill,
Massachusetts, about 1805. It is furnished as the bedroom-
sitting room of a New England merchant prince of the period.
The thin reeded columns with brass bases and capitals on the
mantel, the plaster ornament on the chair rail and chimney
breast, and the fret design of the cornice (copied from the 1792
edition of Pain's *Builder's Companion*) are combined to produce
this notably harmonious early nineteenth-century interior from
north of Boston. It is dominated by what is generally considered to be the finest surviving American bed from this period—
an altogether magnificent joint effort of thoroughly accomplished craftsmen, which descended in the Derby family (FIG.
102). Its cornice, original in conception and decorated in color
and gold, was the combined achievement of John Doggett, a
celebrated looking-glass-frame maker of Roxbury, Massachusetts, and John Ritto Penniman, an ornamental painter who
sometimes worked with Doggett. The bedstead itself was
fashioned in the workshop of Thomas Seymour; the exquisitely

carved details on the front posts are attributed to Thomas Whitman.

A chair with a scroll back and figured-birch panels, a variation of a design from an 1812 London trade manual, is also attributed to the enterprising Seymour workshop. Here too is a handsome example of what Sheraton referred to as a "Gentleman's Secretary." Such a piece, Sheraton wrote, was "intended for a gentleman to write at, to keep his own accounts, and serves as a library." This example (PL. 21) is presumably the work of Nehemiah Adams of Salem, a craftsman who participated in a cooperative enterprise that made fine furniture for export throughout the Atlantic world, even to South Africa and on to India. Secretaries of this kind won special favor among the artisans of northeastern New England and consequently have been termed "Salem secretaries."

A mahogany bureau, or four-drawer chest, with contrasting panels of flaming-birch veneers and what is called a "drop panel" in the center of the skirt is characteristic of the fine cabinetwork produced in and about Portsmouth, New Hampshire. The gracefully contoured bracket feet, also veneered, are of a type described in contemporary references as French feet. These larger pieces are complemented by a washstand made by William Hook of Salem, a small satinwood dressing table, and an easy chair, all also of New England origin.

Richmond Room

Duncan Phyfe's New York establishment produced furniture in a succession of styles almost until the middle of the last century. Examples of his later Federal work are shown in the Richmond room, which features most unusual solid-mahogany wainscoting and door and window units. The woodwork is signed and dated 1811 by one Theo. Nash, "Executor," presumably the joiner. Baseboards are of a stone known as King-of-Prussia marble, quarried only in the Philadelphia area. The room is from a house in Richmond, Virginia.

Two caryatids support the mantel of the marble fireplace installed on one wall. The mantel is ornamented with carved anthemia and other classical motifs and, on a central oval panel above the fireplace opening, a depiction of Hercules resting, club in hand, on the slain Nemean lion. A French gilt-bronze clock on the mantel displays the freestanding figure of George Washington (modeled on a portrait by John Trumbull), and patriotic motifs relating to his fame. The other walls are covered with facsimiles of a colorful French scenic wallpaper – a popular embellishment of Federal American homes from New England to Virginia. First published in 1814 by the Dufour firm of Paris, this paper celebrates The Monuments of Paris (PL. 22). An ornamental plaster rosette in the ceiling is adapted from a design in Asher Benjamin's *The American Builder's Companion*, a widely used reference book published at Boston in 1806.

Among the furniture in this room are a pair of satinwood consoles in a particular version of the Sheraton style that was apparently introduced into America by Phyfe (and copied by others in the New York area). Vase-shaped pedestals, "clover-leaf" tops, and incurving legs whose waterleaf carving matches that on the pedestals are typical of this style. About 1810, according to family tradition, Thomas Cornell Pearsall ordered a large suite of mahogany chairs with "Grecian Cross" legs from Phyfe. These were based on the curule, or folding seat, used by Roman magistrates. A few of the twelve chairs from this set, now owned by the Museum, are shown here, as is a sofa of the same design (FIG. 103). The curule shape appeared in both

FIG. 103.
Sofa, part of a suite made by the workshop of Duncan Phyfe (active 1792-1847), New York City, mahogany, cane, gilt-brass ornament, 1810-1820.

Gift of C. Ruxton Love, Jr., 60.4.1.

French and English pattern books of the early nineteenth century. In the Pearsall chairs, the curves of the legs are repeated in the design of the backs. The seats are covered with a reproduction of the blue Chinese-export silk with which they were originally upholstered.

The later classical style of Phyfe and his New York contemporaries, dating from about 1815 to 1825, reflects an increasing awareness of Greco-Roman architectural forms and decoration as these had been adapted during the Directory, Consulat, and Empire to what the French called *le style antique*. A variety of new publications issued in France and England introduced these to Americans, as did the experienced craftsmen familiar with fashionable taste overseas who continued to immigrate.

Neoclassical Gallery

One of the many highly skilled émigrés, Charles-Honoré Lannuier, who came to New York from France to practice his craft, made two important and elaborate marble-topped pier tables displayed in this gallery (FIG. 104). Taken together, these pieces provide a summary of the rich vocabulary of ornament that characterized American interpretations of the French Empire style. Derived ultimately from classical models, the opulently carved and gilded caryatid and winged-swan supports; hairy paw and dolphin feet; applied ormolu, or gilt-bronze, mounts of classical design; and brass inlays in a Greek-key pattern reflect the exuberant antiquarianism that dominated stylish design of the period.

The work of Michael Allison, another New York furniture maker of the Federal and Empire periods, is often indistinguishable from that of Phyfe, unless labeled or otherwise documented. Fortunately, Allison's label does appear on a small, sensitively conceived desk and worktable with swan-neck lyres, carved eagle-head feet, and tambour-fronted work spaces beneath its drawers and writing surface.

The gallery in which these pieces are installed is square in plan with a high ceiling, typical of neoclassical halls of great houses. It is a composite of diverse architectural and decorative elements. The architraves, baseboards, and a pair of sliding doors, painted to simulate mahogany, are from the summer house of the Halsted family in Rye, New York; the cornice is a reproduction of one from a house on Market Street, New York. Wall paintings simulating ashlar, or dressed rectangular stones, trompe-l'œil swags on panels over the doorways, and the grey-and-white checkerboard marble floor tiles are adaptations from original features in the Alsop house, Middletown, Connecticut.

Benkard Room

A room rescued from a derelict house in Petersburg, Virginia, dating from 1811, serves as a setting for furniture collected over the years by the discriminating Mrs. Harry Horton Benkard and given to the Museum by a group of her friends after her death. The architectural trim of the room itself is enriched by stucco ornament in the form of delicate arabesques, foliage, and other motifs in a manner picturesquely reminiscent of an Adam interior. The central panel of the marble mantel is engagingly carved in a depiction of the classical legend of Leda and the Swan.

FIG. 104.

Pier table, bearing remnants of three labels of Charles-Honoré Lannuier (active New York 1803-1819), New York City, rosewood veneer, mahogany, marble, gilt gesso and verde antique, gilt-bronze mounts, gilded terracotta decoration, c. 1815.

Friends of the American Wing Fund, 68.43.

Baltimore Room

FIG. 105. (OPPOSITE)
One of a set of six square-back chairs, New York City, mahogany, 1795-1810.

Gift of the Members of the Committee of the Bertha King Benkard Memorial Fund, 46.67.

The furniture represents a summary statement of American neoclassical form and ornament and is a striking reminder of the private collector's role in appreciating and preserving American decorative arts. Here are brought together such interesting and varied pieces as a sofa of singular grace with a square back, probably made by the New York firm of Slover and Taylor during the first decade of the last century; and a mahogany and satinwood secretary-bookcase from Baltimore. An inlaid Pembroke, or drop-leaf, table with two shallow leaves, represents a type that gained wide popularity in post-Revolutionary years–nowhere more so than in New York, where this example was made. Their compactness made such small tables suitable for a variety of uses. A pair of Boston Sheraton-style card tables and a set of square-back mahogany New York chairs (FIG. 105) are also on view here. A Brussels carpet copied from an unusual needlework example made in New York State in 1810 covers the floor.

Baltimore Room

A dining room removed from a house built at 913 East Pratt Street, Baltimore, just before the War of 1812 also adjoins the large central gallery. The architectural elements–pilasters, colonettes, and cornice worked in solid pine–are delicate in scale and refined in detail. The relations of the openings in the walls–arched recesses flanking the fireplace, tall windows, and doors–and the wall surfaces with oval panels echoing those in the alcoves and the mantel reveal a studied composition and a restrained elegance typical of the revived classicism of the early Republic.

By the beginning of the nineteenth century the port of Baltimore, commanding the shipping on Chesapeake Bay, had become a principal market town for most of the South and a good portion of Pennsylvania. One European visitor commended the city's "American frankness and French ease." Its rocketing prosperity brought an influx of skilled craftsmen, many from Great Britain, whose work was closer to English models than that of any other American city. Baltimore Federal furniture made conspicuous and colorful use of light-wood inlays and painted glass (*verre églomisé*), often with classical motifs, set into the wood. In addition to these features, the elaborate sideboard

FIRST FLOOR

Baltimore Room

FIG. 106.
Sideboard with knife boxes,
Baltimore or Philadelphia,
mahogany veneer, mahogany,
boxwood, ebony, and satinwood inlays; silver on copper;
églomisé panels, 1795–1815.

Purchase, Joseph Pulitzer Bequest and
Mitchel Taradash Gift, 1945 (45.77.)

here (FIG. 106) has marquetry veneers, inlaid designs of Shef-
field silver and ivory, and attendant knife boxes which have
curved and patterned tambours. This unique piece carries the
local interpretation of the Sheraton style to its extreme expression.

A sectional dining table with eagle inlays and a surrounding
set of square-back Sheraton-style chairs offer further opportunity to study the Baltimore style in furniture, as do a pair of
card tables with satinwood inlays that stand in the arched
recesses (FIG. 107). It is evident that painted-glass decoration

was not exclusively a Baltimore device in the remarkably handsome pair of carved and gilded Massachusetts wall mirrors with églomisé inserts that hang over the card tables (FIG. 108). A French Aubusson carpet and a Waterford glass chandelier add brilliant accents to this colorful interior.

A pair of English Argand lamps with cut-glass reservoirs, Wedgwood bases, and white metal mounts are of a type that represent the first radically improved lighting device in history, a 1783 invention of the Swiss Aimé Argand. The illuminating oil was fed from the elevated reservoir to a tubular wick in a way

FIG. 107.
Card table, Baltimore, mahogany veneer, mahogany, satinwood, sycamore, and holly inlays, 1790-1805.

The Sylmaris Collection, Gift of George Coe Graves, 32.55.4.

that provided both its outer and inner surfaces with air. Both Franklin and Jefferson were in Paris at the time and bought several of the lamps; shortly afterward Washington was using them at Mount Vernon.

FIG. 108.
One of a pair of looking glasses, Boston, gilt gesso on pine and wire, églomisé tablet, 1795–1810.

Sansbury-Mills Fund, 56.46.1.

Early Federal Furniture and Decorative Arts Gallery

On this floor, as on the one above, a separate long gallery along the east side of the building is reserved for the display of furnishings of particular interest. Here most of the material is from Boston's North Shore, an area where superb craftsmen found ample and discriminating patronage. Among the most prominent and versatile of these artisans was Samuel McIntire of Salem, who was a carpenter and a carver working on ships, buildings, and furniture; a designer; an architect; and a musician of sorts. The carved eagle and swags set against a stippled

background on a "Square Sofa" in the Sheraton taste (FIG. 109) are in McIntire's individual style, as are the motifs carved on the Hepplewhite chairs. The latter are from a set made for the Derby family of Salem.

McIntire designed the house of Elias Haskct Derby, "more like a palace than the dwelling of an American merchant," according to a visitor from Baltimore, and worked on many of the details that distinguished that short-lived structure. Apparently, all that remains of the once-celebrated building is a

FIG. 109.
Sofa, carving attributed to Samuel McIntire (active c. 1782-1811), Salem, Massachusetts, mahogany, 1800-1810.
Fletcher Fund, 26.207.

171

**Early Federal Furniture
and Decorative Arts
Gallery**

FIG. 110.

Tambour desk, by Reuben
Swift (active 1802-1820s), New
Bedford, Massachusetts,
mahogany, burl walnut; flame-
grain birch, tulip, and maple
veneers, c. 1809.

Bequest of Cecile L. Mayer, 1962
(62.171.6).

PLATE 21. (OPPOSITE)
Gentleman's secretary, attributed to Nehemiah Adams
(active c. 1790-1840), Salem,
Massachusetts, mahogany
veneer, mahogany, and satinwood inlay, 1800-1810.

Purchase, Gift of Mrs. Russell Sage,
Bequest of Ethel Yocum, Bequest of
Charlotte E. Hoadley, and Rogers
Fund, by exchange, 1971.9.

mantelpiece carved with classic scenes and motifs, shown here.

Until a very few years ago when the Museum acquired a desk
bearing his label (FIG. 110), Reuben Swift of New Bedford had
been all but forgotten. The desk is an original and sophisticated
interpretation of prevailing styles. With its richly contrasting
woods in plain and marquetry surfaces, it is enough to establish
him as a cabinetmaker of imagination and rare competence.

One of the most graceful and distinctively American chairs
ever made, a type with a high upholstered back and open arms,
was known to contemporaries as a "lolling" chair. Sometimes in
this country, for no known reason, it was also called a Martha
Washington chair. The example here was made in Portsmouth,

New Hampshire, a town that in the Federal period boasted a fashionable (and conservative) society second to none in New England. A Sheraton desk and bookcase with pointed arches surrounded by delicate reeded molding and bird's-eye maple and mahogany veneers is attributed to the Boston workshop of Thomas Seymour.

Expert craftsmanship in all mediums abounded in New England. The clockmakers of the region were unsurpassed, as a group of timepieces of different kinds testify. Clocks made in other areas, showing some regional differences in case designs, are included, although the basic pre-Revolutionary form of the tall clock persisted for many decades. An example of what is called the "Roxbury" type, made by the well-known Massachusetts clockmaker Aaron Willard, Jr. (FIG. 111), has the painted dial, fluted corner columns on the waist, bracket feet, arched head with scrollwork, and vase-shaped brass finials characteristic of his work. Other clocks from different states share the same general appearance but vary in the treatment of details.

During the Federal period, American clockmaking took a vital new turn with the development of small and relatively inexpensive wall and shelf clocks of a strictly native character. What is known as the Massachusetts shelf clock, made in a variety of designs over the years, remained popular from the Revolutionary period until several decades after the war. The case of this type of timepiece consists of a box on a box, the upper one housing the mechanism, the lower one accommodating the weights and pendulum, as shown here in several examples by Aaron Willard, David Wood, and others. Around 1802, Simon Willard invented his "Improved Patent Time Piece." With is gilt case, painted-glass panels, delicately fashioned hands, and, importantly, its precise workmanship and fine proportions, this eight-day banjo clock immediately won well-deserved success. Despite Willard's patent, it was quickly copied by other makers. Twenty years later Willard patented his "Eddystone Lighthouse Alarm Time Piece," named after the famous structure built upon the Eddystone Rocks near Plymouth, England. This model was also quickly copied, although no two surviving examples are exactly alike.

About this time, Connecticut Yankee clockmakers were initiating cheap clocks whose works consisted of interchangeable

PLATE 22. (OPPOSITE)
Wallpaper panel showing a scene with milkmaid and bathers, Arc du Carrousel and Palais Mazarin in background, reproduced from Dufour's "Monuments of Paris" wallpaper of 1814.

Photograph courtesy of The Twigs, Boston, Massachusetts.

FIG. 111.
Shelf clock, works by Aaron Willard (active 1780-1823), Boston, mahogany, brass ornament, 1790-1800.

The Sylmaris Collection, Gift of George Coe Graves, 30.120.65.

Early Federal Furniture and Decorative Arts Gallery

machine-made parts produced in an assembly-line system. Pillar-and-scroll clocks were among the earliest, represented here by an example made by Seth Thomas of Plymouth, Connecticut—a name still familiar to clock buyers today. The clock stands on slender feet, and is decorated with flanking pillars, a broken-arch pediment, brass finials, and a painted-glass panel showing a view of Mount Vernon. Veneer and mortising mills and circular saws had reduced the cost of the cases. Some American clocks of modest size and price were winning ready markets around the world.

Second Floor, New Wing

2

3

→ 2 ⚤

2 | ⚤

M

1 |

Old Wing | New Wing

Paintings and Sculpture: 18th Century to Late 19th Century

Late Colonial Period Decorative Arts, 1730-90

Silver, Pewter, Glass, and Ceramics

201 Late 19th-Century Decorative Arts
202 Silver and Pewter
203 Glass and Ceramics
204 18th-Century Furniture and Decorative Arts
205 Philadelphia Chippendale Furniture
206 Van Rensselaer Hall
207 Marmion Room
208 Verplanck Room

Joan Whitney Payson Galleries: Paintings and Sculpture

217 18th Century
218 Late 18th — Early 19th Century
219 1812 until 1840
220 Early Hudson River School
221 Late Hudson River School
222 Winslow Homer
223 Selected Paintings, 1780-1880, and Emanuel Leutze, *Washington Crossing the Delaware*, 1851
224 Post-Civil War Realism, Trompe l'Oeil Painting, Western Art, and Visionary Painting

Elevators
E1 Stops in New Wing
E2 Stops in New Wing ⚤

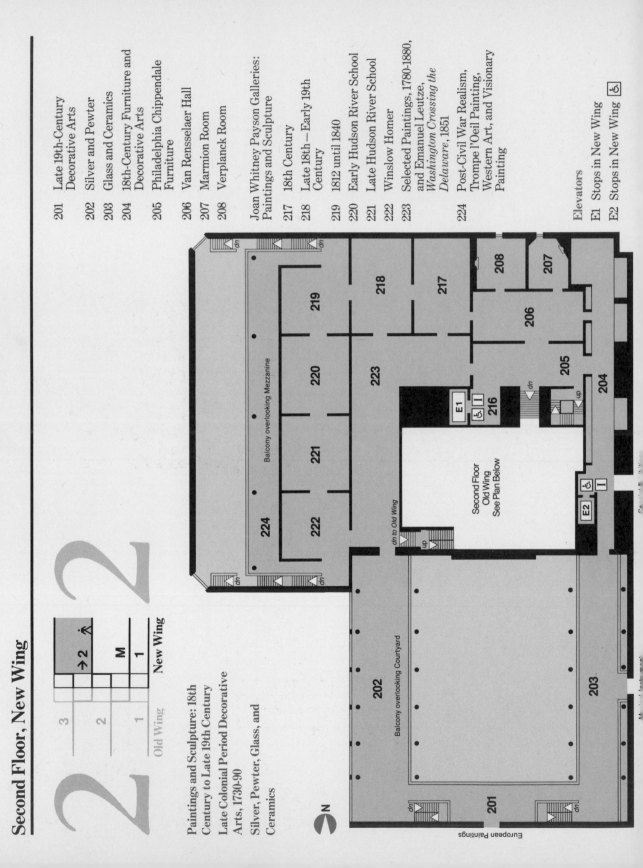